FRANCO ZEFFIRELLI'S JESUS

FRANCO ZEFFIRELLI'S

JESUS

A Spiritual Diary

Franco Zeffirelli

Translated from the Italian by Willis J. Egan, S.J.

1817

Harper & Row, Publishers, San Francisco
Cambridge, Hagerstown, New York, Philadelphia
London, Mexico City, São Paulo, Singapore, Sydney

FIRST U.S. EDITION

Library of Congress Cataloging in Publication Data

Zeffirelli, Franco.
  FRANCO ZEFFIRELLI'S JESUS

  Translation of: Il mio Gesù.
  1. Gesù. [Motion picture] I. Title.
PN1997.G443Z413   1984   791.43'72   84-47890
ISBN 0-06-069780-6

84 85 86 87 88 10 9 8 7 6 5 4 3 2 1

Contents

Introduction to the English Edition

This book is a collection of my memories, backed by random notes and letters that I wrote during the planning and making of my film on the life of Jesus. As such I realize how incomplete the whole thing is.

It can only be.

There are so many more flashes of the vivid—sometimes funny, sometimes near tragic—and deeply moving moments of those wonderful, uplifting days that have come flooding back. I have largely resisted the temptation to add them to this English edition, and the book closely follows the Italian version published in 1977.

It is a fact that since its writing, I have been seeing this book in different perspectives. How can I explain it? For a start, I wrote it when I was still editing the film in London, working around the clock as we wanted to release it for Easter, fast approaching. When the publishers, Sperling and Kupfer, asked me to write about its making and the reasons why, it didn't seem such a difficult task. Every day I was exposed to my memories etched on the film flicking through the editing moviola, and I breathed again the air of the locations that made so many visions a reality.

The result became a sort of unintentional "literary" diary of a journey. And as I re-read it now, this surprises me. The only form of writing I have been used to is setting down shooting scripts or stories in treatment form.

The book has had a definite "stock-taking" effect on me. I was able to confirm that my life (1) before making the film, (2) during my thinking about it, and (3) with the making of it and after had valid roots and reasons. Each of these various stages led up to changes in my very thinking, with revelations that struck me with the force of a hurricane.

I was a typical "lazy Catholic," who accepted the awesome mystery of our faith as a matter of course. Like most of us, I hadn't read very much of the Gospels. I vaguely knew certain sections, completely out of context, as if they were an assortment of pieces from a jigsaw puzzle cut out of the general tradition. In the making of the film, the pieces began to come together, recomposing the story of our Lord into one giant, harmonious, exciting fresco.

In studying and understanding better the teachings of Jesus, I realized how essential it was to put his words into the historical and social context of his times, which became a major purpose in the making of the film. Jesus knew his audience well. He never spoke to the people as a virtuoso, just for the sake of it. He often repeated the same concepts to many different kinds of people—to the fishermen, the Pharisees, the peasants, the intellectuals, to the rich and the poor. For all and each of them he found images and words familiar to them.

When the film was shown there was much controversy about the setting of the parable of the Prodigal Son. I felt that the conflict between Peter and Matthew should come to a head in the house of the sinner. Here Jesus broke through to the hearts of the people with his story of love and forgiveness, which convinced not only Matthew but also the somewhat aggressive Peter—and all of this in a house that his followers were convinced would contaminate and defile them all, including the Master.

So many other events in the Gospels stand out with astonishing lucidity, but none so clearly as those told by Saint John. It is evident that he was really there, as a young man, with Jesus during some of the most dramatic and significant episodes of Jesus' life. He recounts them with such wonderful verbal imagery, almost as if he were a supremely gifted screenwriter! So many scenes reported by him we simply filmed directly. I only had to pass his words to the actors, who, by speaking them as written, produced the most dramatic and poignant effects.

My profession is one of communication. I feel I have never misused my responsibility as director by presenting anything offensive to my audience, and I have always questioned deeply my motives before mounting any project. This camera, with its lenses that look at what you do with stark exactitude, is a frightening witness. It has the potential to present the results of your efforts to untold millions—from a peasant in Japan, a student in Texas, a rich man in Milan, to an aborigine in Australia.

During the preparation of the film, Pope Paul VI expressed his awareness of the power of this medium in an audience with me when he said:

God is offering to you the language of today, this new way of communicating with people. If you had lived two hundred years ago you would probably have written a book or painted the story in murals. . . . But perhaps the most effective medium of today to communicate . . . to work as a missionary, is television and cinema. There is so much you can do through them to enrich . . . or to impoverish man. . . .

Then he said:

But this is only the beginning, remember . . .

Pope Paul used this last significant phrase again, in an unprecedented reference to any television program, during the Sunday Blessing from his window before a crowded Saint Peter's Square on April 10, 1977.

Tonight you are going to see an example of a fine use that can be made of the new ways of communication that God is offering man. But keep in mind that, whatever good feelings and effects this experience will have on you, this must only mark the beginning of your search for God. Only the beginning . . .

It seems that, up to now, 750 million people have seen the film throughout the world. With the massive increase in videotape and other forms of distribution, the figure is more likely over a billion. I only wish I had the space to reproduce in detail some of the letters from every kind, nationality, race, and class of person telling me of the impact that the film has had on their lives. Collectively they would make a book in themselves.

Here, in essence, are three examples of the kinds of letters that remain strongly in my mind.

The first was from a young Japanese girl living near San Francisco. She was in utter despair because of the recent death of both her parents. She had no other relatives, and the man she was to marry had just left her for another girl. She felt there was nothing left but to end it all. She sat in front of the television before taking her sleeping pills. The program just happened to be the first part of *Jesus of Nazareth.* As the story progressed, she became so involved as to be distracted from her state of despair, and with each succeeding episode, her sense of futility faded.

After the last part of the film, with a new feeling of faith and hope, she wrote to me in a quaint, broken English telling her story —and enclosed her sleeping pills in the envelope.

Another letter came from France and expressed a concern that must be felt by many families today. A father and mother with two teenage children wrote of their progressive sense of alienation from them. The children kept very much to themselves and didn't seem to want even their company. Conversation and communication was reduced to a minimum, if there was any at all.

As the first episode of the film began, the children drifted in, sitting listlessly in front of the television set. At the end of the screening there was an even more marked silence than before. But somehow it was different. It was after the second part that the eldest boy began to ask his father something about the background of the Gospels. The girl joined in, and soon a lively discussion developed. By the end of the whole film, the desire to find out more about Jesus had been instilled into the whole family. But the most important part of the expression of thanks from the parents was that the film had brought them together again as a family with a warmth and respect previously missing.

And as a final example, there was a letter from a Milanese mother expecting her fourth child in a family already heavily strained by inadequate housing and all sorts of financial problems. Both she and her husband had seriously considered arranging an abortion, as distressing as it would have been for them.

The film so deeply affected their children that the parents were profoundly touched by the unexpected joy that radiated from their faces. They realized that with all their hardship, in no way could they prevent a fourth child from being part of that joy.

Three years later I received a charming Christmas family photo of the proud parents surrounded by *five* happy and healthy children!

At the end of this book I say something to the effect that, if only one person in the world is moved for the good by my film, then all effort and sacrifice will have been worthwhile.

Time—and such letters as those I have just outlined—have fulfilled my hopes more than I dreamed possible.

And more than I deserve.

FRANCO ZEFFIRELLI
Rome 1984

CHAPTER 1

A Conspiracy of Events

After completing my film *Jesus of Nazareth* I thought long and deeply about all the events surrounding its making and my involvement. I became convinced that at a certain moment in my life I was engulfed by a "conspiracy of happenings." The phrase is apt, as it stops me from believing, prompted by my instinctive pride and vanity, that I alone was singled out by some inexplicable design. Yet I may still allow Romeo to speak for me when he says: "But he, that hath the steerage of my course, direct my sail."

The last film I had directed dealt with the youthful years of Saint Francis of Assisi. The joy in its making left me quite satisfied, and I felt that I had said all that my modest faith permitted me to say. A priest who is very dear to me warned that when you begin to involve yourself in godly matters it is terribly difficult to return to mundane trivialities. Yet I felt with this film I had closed the door on my availability to treat themes that in one way or another would concern faith, religion, or the spiritual vocation.

In fact, with no effort at all I immediately became involved in an entirely different direction. As Saint Francis appeared on the screen, I began to think about the story of Marguerite Gauthier, or Alphonsine Duplessis, the courtesan beloved and glorified by Alexandre Dumas.

My priest friend smiled when I told him this, saying how happy he was that I had continued along the path of that certain "calling." He pointed out that even the story of the poor prostitute of Paris was along the line I could not abandon. "Don't you see that you are pursuing the story of Mary Magdalene?"

At the same time I was thinking about another Shakespearean

subject (following *Taming of the Shrew* and *Romeo and Juliet*) and felt a strong attachment for *Much Ado About Nothing* after directing it at London's National Theatre. In no way did it seem to have anything to do with the "current" in which, according to my priest friend, I was destined to be at that moment of my life.

With the excited interest in *Brother Sun,* the story of Saint Francis of Assisi, around the world, proposals for films with a religious theme descended on my desk. I turned them down, still convinced that I had said all that I possibly could in the field of religious movies and would never return to them.

I looked for other avenues, other ideas, but could decide on nothing. A couple of years went by—'71 and '72—marked by increasing unrest. I returned to the theater, which, like a mother, has always taken me into her arms in moments of discomfort and confusion.

Then came the commuting between Rome, London, and New York trying to put together some film project. With all the interesting offers, I still desperately needed something that would really be mine.

It was in the autumn of 1973 that my agent rang to tell me of a vast project for which my name had been proposed: an important television production that would also be a significant film on the life of Jesus. I told him not to waste too much time in thinking that I would accept and that, anyway, they would soon find someone else.

Then, slowly and strangely, ideas evoked by these proposals took shape in the form of a film project on Dante's *Inferno*—an idea already cherished by me even before the film on Saint Francis. I first seriously thought about it at Moscow in 1970 on the anniversary of the poet's death.

I remember being so furious to see the Soviet men of culture preparing to celebrate the event with a fervor lacking in Italy—even in Florence. It was in this state of mind that I proposed to shoot, along with the Soviets, a film on the *Divine Comedy,* at the same time deciding to produce it.

It was a mistake—a clear mistake—and yet at the time I couldn't see it; I had been so affected by the singular enthusiasm of the people. I even went to Yugoslavia checking out exteriors.

The Dante film was not religious, of course, but somehow seemed to mark a return to certain motifs that I had begun to develop in the film on Saint Francis—the degrees of crisis in a man torn in the eternal dilemma of good and evil. And all seemed ready to go ahead.

With the *Inferno* project so strongly in mind, I started working in London with Laurence Olivier on De Filippo's *Saturday, Sunday and Monday*. Suddenly a call from my agent came again with that offer to direct the film about Jesus:

"Are you sure you're not interested? Let's think it over, because you are on top of the list of directors selected by the producers."

He took that sort of flattering tone in his attempts to entice me into accepting. He was right when he added that here was a project greater and more ambitious than English or Italian television had ever conceived.

Actually, the idea was originally thought of in Italy by Pier Emilio Gennarini, Emanuele Milano, and Fabiano Fabiani, three Catholics of great faith and deep evangelical culture. It then rebounded in England, and from there Sir Lew Grade took it over.

Immediately there was the expected resistance on a political level in the RAI (Italian television network) and other internal opposition from a number of people because, by their standards, my Catholicism was not objective enough. Yet those same people fervently supported the candidacy of Bergman. So typical of our way of doing things—that is, the Italians supporting a foreign director rather than an Italian backed by the Americans and the English. Even at this point I said, "No, let's not even speak about it! I have to make *The Inferno*, and this is already fully occupying my mind." I admit that I also felt a sort of fear—a refusal to bear the spiritual strain along with the responsibilities that a film about Jesus would have laid on me.

Then began what I can only call the hecatomb, the slaughter of the innocents, the mowing-down—a grotesque succession of reversals and collapsing projects. It almost felt as though lines were being drawn for the Jesus film to find its way to me and I would be forced into a position of accepting.

First of all, *The Inferno* was canceled in January of 1973 because the production lacked the expertise that was indispensable to me for an enterprise of this sort.

And so, with six months' work just blown away in the wind, nothing remained for me but to throw myself body and soul into a previous idea—a free adaption of Dumas's *Camille* starring Liza Minelli. I wanted to set it in a later Paris than the Dumas period, as Miss Minelli did not quite strike me as a romantic character but as one of those plain-pretty women of Manet or Degas—not to mention Toulouse-Lautrec—a woman typical of the decline of the Belle Epoque.

I was thinking about a story of the son of a famous politician desperately in love with a Parisian chanteuse, set in the period just after the Dreyfus Affair, then from this to the story's sensational scandal.

Everything was going well, the setting, characters, and plot. Producer Grimaldi had offered to finance the scenario. Then right in the middle of it all—frantic traveling between London and New York and location hunting in Paris—along came another telegram from Sir Lew Grade: "I must see you. URGENT."

It is hard to say no to Sir Lew, but I tried once more to withdraw from the project: "Let's do the Medici," I suggested, even though I had already done two films with a Renaissance setting. "Or let me explore the sacred experiment of the Jesuits in South America, the famous Paraguay Reductions. But I cannot shoot a film on Christ, do you understand?"

"But why not?" Sir Lew asked.

"Why should I?" I countered.

A bit later, because of a series of delayed decisions, we couldn't have Miss Minelli, who was by now contracted for several concerts. And so, in the spring of 1973, I found myself in an unusual situation. I had no project to work on.

Fortune was weaving, slowly but surely, its own web. The plot thickened.

It was indeed Sir Lew Grade who roused me out of my lack of interest:

"Franco, don't renounce this film on Jesus. Think it over well—without commitment, of course. There is so much in it that is right for you, above all, a rediscovery of the Gospels in the light of more recent historical studies and an act of love for Christ. An Italian Catholic director is what we want and, moreover, one who is known and respected in all countries, particularly in the Anglo-Saxon world."

I had seen all the films on Jesus and felt that the most beautiful was the French director Duvivier's from the late thirties, for which he shot exteriors entirely in Provence. A bare hour and a half of film. It was obvious to me that in such a short time you cannot tell the vast story recorded in the Gospels and involve a didactical text, as it were. It was this challenge, in part, that convinced me I should accept. Here was the chance of accomplishing, thanks to the six or more hours of television, a grand enterprise that could turn out to be useful somehow to everybody—to believer as well as non-believer.

Besides, for a year and a half, these proposals had kept me thinking. I had refused them, yes, but I had not given up reading, studying, and working around the figure of Christ and discussing it with specialists. And so, little by little, I came to the conviction that this insistence, this continual return of the offer to produce a project of such scope about Christ, must have a meaning, some deep significance.

I became more and more aware that I had at my disposal, within a time span not usually permitted in the cinema, a subject of incomparable worth, a subject that too often had given life to films reproachable for their empty rhetoric. For the most part the stories were saccharine, distorted, hypercritical productions, many of them analogous to the Fascist and Nazi films or to the Russian films under Stalin and Lenin. No doubt it was a good time to give Christ back a little of his own.

There was another point that came sharply to mind, again in the direct arguments from Sir Lew: "Also consider this, Franco. I have already decided to produce the film, and though I want you to do it, if you don't, someone else will, and perhaps you will have lost a unique opportunity to tell the story of Christ in a new way to our generation."

He continued, clinching his points.

"The time allotted for the television script will allow you to develop the narrative in unprecedented depth. At a moment of universal crisis in the West, a crisis of all traditional values and of all ideals, with this film we can perhaps remind people what they are foolishly and wickedly losing."

While all of these pressures were urging me to accept there came an event that I have always kept deep in my subconcious and that had a greater influence on my decision to go ahead than anything I have mentioned so far. It had become for me so profound in its truth that I could never openly discuss it at the time, though I knew that Sir Lew Grade, himself a Jew, would have been moved and reassured to know of it.

It was a statement of unprecedented courage by the Church in Vatican Council II, lead by Pope Paul VI in 1965, on the Jewish responsibility for the death of Christ.

The clarity of it had impressed me with an inner feeling that some day I might be guided by its strength and perhaps even present a vital, new overall approach in a film on the story of Jesus and his relationship with his people.

I went to the Vatican library and read again the very words that made that message so memorable.

For those who may have at the time underrated its significance, I make no apology for quoting, almost in full, paragraph 4 in the declaration *Nostra Aetate* ("Our Times") on Judaism:

As this Sacred Synod searches into the mystery of the Church it remembers the bond that spiritually ties the people of the New Covenant to Abraham's stock.

Thus the Church of Christ acknowledges that, according to God's saving design, the beginnings of her faith and her election are found already among the Patriarchs, Moses and the Prophets. She professes that all who believe in Christ—Abraham's sons according to faith—are included in the same Patriarch's call, and likewise that the salvation of the Church is mysteriously foreshadowed by the chosen people's exodus from the land of bondage. The Church, therefore, cannot forget that she received the revelation of the Old Testament through the people with whom God in His inexpressible mercy concluded the Ancient Covenant. Nor can she forget that she draws sustenance from the root of the well-cultivated olive tree onto which have been grafted the wild shoots, the Gentiles. Indeed, the Church believes that by His cross Christ Our Peace reconciled Jews and Gentiles, making both one in Himself. . . .

She also recalls that the Apostles, the Church's mainstay and pillars, as well as most of the early disciples who proclaimed Christ's Gospel to the world, sprang from the Jewish people. . . .

Since the spiritual patrimony common to Christians and Jews is thus so great, this Sacred Synod wants to foster and recommend that mutual understanding and respect which is the fruit, above all, of biblical and theological studies as well as of fraternal dialogues.

True, the Jewish authorities and those who followed their lead pressed for the death of Christ; still, what happened in His passion cannot be charged against all the Jews, without distinction, then alive, nor against the Jews of today. Although the Church is the new people of God, the Jews should not be presented as rejected by God or accursed, as if this followed from the Holy Scriptures. All should see to it, then, that in catechetical work or in the preaching of the word of God they do not teach anything that does not conform to the truth of the Gospel and the spirit of Christ.

Furthermore, in her rejection of every persecution against any man, the Church, mindful of the patrimony she shares with the Jews and moved by the spiritual love of the Gospel and not by political reasons, decries hatred, persecutions, manifestations of anti-semitism, directed against Jews at any time and by anyone.

Besides, as the Church has always held and holds now, Christ underwent His passion and death freely, because of the sins of men and out of infinite love, in order that all may reach salvation. It is, therefore, the burden of the Church's preaching to proclaim the cross of Christ as the sign of God's all-embracing love and as the fountain from which every grace flows. . . .

No foundation therefore remains for any theory or practice that leads to discrimination between man and man or people and people, so far as their human dignity and the rights flowing from it are concerned.

The Church reproves, as foreign to the mind of Christ, any discrimination against men or harassment of them because of their race, colour, condition in life, or religion. On the contrary, following in the footsteps of the holy Apostles Peter and Paul, this Sacred Synod ardently implores the Christian faithful to maintain good fellowship among the nations (1 Pet 2:12), and, if possible, to live for their part in peace with all men, so that they may truly be sons of the Father who is in heaven.

The reading of this document settled the matter for me. Now I felt a sort of moral responsibility to make the film. To turn down this moment could only bring an incurable regret that would overtake me long into the future.

I wired my acceptance to Sir Lew Grade.

It was the winter of 1973, a few days before Christmas.

CHAPTER 2

In Search of Nazareth, the Temple, and Other Things

I revisited it all, walking again the places Christ and his apostles had trodden, but I became bitterly disillusioned. Only Bethlehem has a beautiful Byzantine church, a testimony to a time and to the days when civilization still built masterpieces instinctively, automatically.

Nazareth is a travesty. The French built there in the twenties the Church of the Annunciation, the ugliest and most cluttered structure you could imagine, a product of one of the most infamous periods of religious architecture ever.

Then, in and around the holy places of Jerusalem, a forest of shops has sprung up where "souvenirs" are sold. In the Church of the Holy Sepulcher, violent strife has broken out among three different religious groups, all residing there and all of them official custodians of the place. The Orthodox have the actual area of the Sepulcher; the Franciscans have their own sector; and a Coptic order has custody of the place of the Crucifixion. Each group in turn harasses the others meaninglessly.

And so the ancient basilica is crumbling to pieces. The Orthodox group mistakes the word "restore" with "rebuild," and are doing just that—horribly. The Franciscans protest in vain while they go ahead restoring their areas according to respectable criteria. The others only want to tear it down and rebuild it haphazardly.

It was a considerable shock to find that many of these most sacred holy places are utterly lacking in religious atmosphere—everybody shouting, traffic noises, and the Israeli police moving

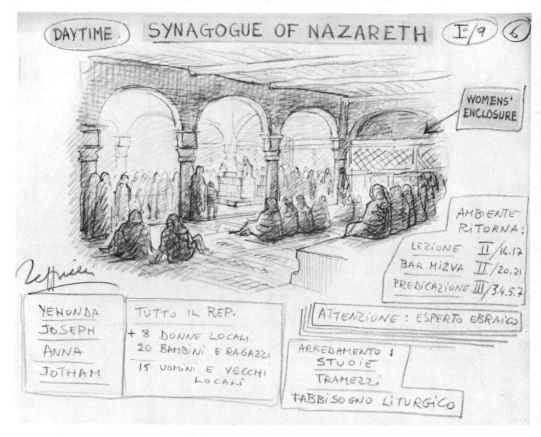

about constantly. An example is the public telephone set up next to the Holy Sepulcher. It works just like all other public phones—miserably. Whoever uses it has to shout to make himself heard, thereby preventing the faithful from any attempt at prayer or meditation.

A small opening, a tomb covered with gold, tassels, and all kinds of lamps, encrustations that have accumulated for centuries—that's the Holy Sepulcher today, a place bereft of any remnant of the world in the time of Jesus. The sad fact is that the character of successive generations—of Arabs, who were the custodians of architectural style, and of the previous Jews—has been completely eradicated during the past thirty years. The Israeli authorities have made sure of this by razing to the ground all homes abandoned by the Arabs.

For their part, the Arabs erred in abandoning Palestine. They were most ill inspired by fellow Arabs with unenlightened political motives. Had they remained in Palestine they could have at least confronted the dominant Jews with more evident claims and possibly built together with them a peaceful state.

But he who walks away often loses his place forever. It is the lesson of history.

There are, then, none of the holy places in the Israeli sector, and the little that remains is adulterated. I also explored much of the landscape—the beautiful desert of Judea that slopes to the Dead Sea. This area still remains untouched, especially near Jericho, though the town itself preserves little of its past and now resembles a sort of Montecatini.

Jordan has remained somewhat untouched because it is a boundary line and still a matter of contention. No one could think of building there. Little communities still appear, such as Nablus, I think the name was, that consist only of a few isolated dwellings. But these Palestinian communities go back for thousands of years.

Nazareth has kept nothing of its ancient character except for the fountain where Arab women still go to draw water. Otherwise everything is modern, and the houses of worship are undistinguished by any architectual nobility, as I have already said and won't tire of repeating.

Going back to Tiberias, now transformed into a "fun resort" with huge hotels "equipped with every comfort," one comes, at the northeast corner, to the Golan Heights, a vigorously contested military zone, absolutely shut off and therefore untouched.

From this point one can see the Sea of Galilee, stretching in a beautiful blue haze that for the moment made me think of going ahead and shooting the scenes of Peter on those shores. Unfortunately there wasn't even a corner suitable for reconstructing Capernaum. The Franciscans were conducting excavations there and had discovered a synagogue and three successive levels of a fishermen's village. It was clearly a city of some importance at one time and certainly a center of commerce. It was a gateway to Syria—Damascus, where the Roman legions were stationed.

The Romans were naturally loathed, yet with the construction of dikes and magnificent aqueducts, they made many desert areas fertile. So did the Arabs later, in the centuries of their splendor. The simple restoration of the ancient systems has in many cases allowed the Israelis to irrigate vast areas, bringing to life plantations abandoned for centuries.

I also thoroughly toured Jordan, with its sadly dispersed people —beautiful people so right for certain needs of the film. But communication was impossible. I went to Syria, where you can find, near the border of Turkey, primitive villages that could evoke a feeling of Nazareth, of Galilee.

But everywhere I ran into difficulties of all kinds.

I returned to Israel across Allenby Bridge, the sole umbilical cord between it and Jordan. We traveled by car escorted by military vehicles up to the meeting place near the bridge. We had to cross on foot, assisted by porters, leaving behind the Jordanian gun-mounts with their machine guns, mortars, and other weapons all protected by sandbags.

When we reached the opposite bank, where the Israeli flag was flying, an Israeli delegation led by the Minister of Communications welcomed me. He was a most courteous man with a completely European mentality and manner.

I had already been in Israel years before when I put on *Falstaff* and *An Italian Girl in Algiers,* conducted by Guilini at the Mann Auditorium in Tel Aviv. But that was in '59 and '62—a completely different political situation. Somehow, so were the people.

The minister looked at me sympathetically but couldn't stop himself from saying: "It's a pity you come here for a project like this."

"I want you to know," I replied, "that I am above all a lover of truth and in no way partisan. Furthermore, I will tell you one of my inmost convictions. I am basically as much a Hebrew as you are!"

The astonished reaction of my interpreter gave me the chance to better clarify my thought.

"You see, we Christians, too, like you and the Arabs, are all sons of Abraham."

"Yes, yes," he went on, slightly confused, "but you are shooting the story of Christ, and usually when it is told in your medium, our danger is rekindled."

I replied: "I assure you that I don't only wish to re-evoke the story of Christ but also the tragedy of the blaming of the Jewish people, which should no longer exist. I want to clarify the reasons that were behind your ancestors' decisions and—within my film— help all to understand them."

My mind was instinctively dwelling on the words of Pope Paul VI's declaration *Nostra Aetate,* which had become my deepest motivation for making the film.

I was looking for a solution for the setting of the Temple—the great Temple of Jerusalem. Unfortunately, the most superb examples of architecture in the Arab world are found only in Cairo. The impressive mosques of the first centuries after Mohammed are huge, splendid edifices originally derived from Hebrew architecture and design, completely free from tinsel and images. The grandeur of the Jerusalem Temple was created by spacious courtyards, enormous cloisters, and sparkling fountains. These are features that can be found in Islamic architecture, particularly in the mosques surrounded by courtyards, the largest central one enhanced on every side by a forest of columns. It is a place conducive to prayer or study.

When I arrived in Cairo I immediately became fascinated by those magnificent edifices, to the point of deciding to shoot the Jerusalem sequences there, particularly the scenes of Herod and Pilate. But although the Egyptian authorities are quick to welcome large motion picture undertakings and eager to bring back productions of any kind into their country, when it comes to using their sacred places or representing the person of a prophet by an actor (and Muslims consider Jesus a prophet), you expose yourself to the peril of many hindrances even though you have permission from Sadat and the Grand Mufti. In fact, according to their law, any fervent Muslim, indignant at seeing a holy place violated, profaned with machinery, lamps, make-believe Jews, handcarts, animals, can step in and say: "I forbid you in the name of the Prophet to continue this work. I order you all to leave." And you have to leave. There is no intervention of authority that can oppose and countermand the order. A film about Mohammed that they were shooting secretly at that time in Morocco was suspended by the intervention of some intransigent religious individuals determined to cut off the work in the name of the Prophet. Even the king of Morocco had to yield and throw them all out, though the troupe, including the director, were all Arabs. Strangely, the project was then inherited by Quaddafi, perhaps simply to show his scorn for his Morrocan colleagues. Who knows?

And so we couldn't have the calm or guarantee that we could

bring the work to its conclusion. I couldn't blank from my mind the horror of suddenly having to stop work because of a single believer's demand after having brought in machinery, costumes, and extras; constructed props; and perhaps shot a few scenes, which would then be useless.

Also, much had to be done scenographically. Significant alterations had to be made to mask Arabic features that were too evident, in order to bring the architecture back to the time of Christ. In spite of the problems, I was very reluctant to abandon these locations because the sites in Cairo are unique in the world.

From all this searching, a certain structure remained in my mind, the mosque of Tulun in the heart of Cairo, the most grandiose mosque of Islam. It is not the Turkish type derived from the church of Santa Sophia in Constantinople (in Cairo there was only one such, built in the past century) but the other type, Islamic, and modeled after the style of the Temple in Jerusalem. There is another famous one at Kerouan in Tunisia.

I kept in mind the conformation and order of the Tulun mosque when my architect, Gianni Quaranta, and I worked on the reconstruction of the Temple. For this location I chose the fortress of Monastir on the Tunisian coast, which in a way reproduced the Tower of Antonius. I was guided by a little model of the Temple that is on a hill in Jerusalem. It is beautifully done, and it has as a natural backdrop the lovely green plain of Judea. People enjoy photographing it and creating special effects to make it appear absolutely real.

The Temple had a great central courtyard with 350 granite columns, the walls covered with cedar of Lebanon and adorned with gold and silver, embellishments that Herod added to ingratiate himself with the Jews and make them forget that he, their king, was only half-Jewish.

This reconstruction at Monastir, by our production schedule, could be used in the second phase of our filming. While they were building it I was already shooting in Morocco.

Morocco is one of the most beautiful countries in the world. It is there that nature's fantasy has been prodigal to the point of bringing together the landscapes of the entire Mediterranean. To begin with there is the Atlas chain of mountains as high as the Alps cutting across the country like an immense granite barrier. It separates the country from the desert and stands as a wondrous natural watershed—a mountain range of nine hundred kilometers that terminates in Algeria. Its highest stretch, rich and fanciful, peaks in Morocco. On the spurs and heights snow remains for a long time. It is a reservoir that sends streams to the south toward the desert, rivers that create and nourish an exuberant vegetation before vanishing into the aridity of the Sahara's sands. Streams to the north support agriculture and produce a land as green and beautiful as Tuscany.

At Meknes, one of the four imperial cities, together with Rabat, Marrakech, and Fez, I found splendid medieval edifices built by the Moors on their return from Spain. These structures reminded me of those in Andalusia—hidden gardens, vast, deep, true Gardens of Allah. The inhabitants, mostly Berbers, are a fiery people. They are not Arabs but Phoenicians, with Semitic, not Hamite, features.

And yet even there I could not find Nazareth—my Nazareth— a place that in any way resembled the Nazareth of my imagination —a Nazareth such as I had meticulously designed for my production team.

Finally, on the day of my departure for Europe there was again a mysterious sign, this time from a glance at a map of the ruins of Volubilis, the remains of one of the greatest African cities of the Roman period. With a few hours on hand before departure, we decided to visit the ruins.

Along the way, there were many people coming and going, a multitude on the move. What was this all about? Then I was told that they were going to Moulay Idriss, a holy place named after a famous ascetic, a disciple of Mohammed, an apostle of the Muslim faith in Morocco who had died there centuries ago at an advanced age. His village is gently couched in green and is a picturesque, lovely settlement of houses that reminded me of certain landscapes around the southern Apennines.

Continuing on toward Volubilis, I suddenly saw on my right a tiny white town, simple and bare, that overlooked the valley, similar in every way to the green valley of Galilee. Captivated by the view, I decided to go up and take a look at the little town before going to the ruins. When there I found myself looking at the very place I had imagined. Here was my dream of Nazareth.

Then a frenzy seized me, an overwhelming excitement. I feverishly began photographing the whole area, at the same time examining every nook and cranny. In a state of total exaltation I forgot all about visiting the ruins of Volubilis. It was an ungrateful lapse, as it was the idea of this "tourist" visit that led me to find my Nazareth!

I returned to Rome with my heart relieved of a very heavy burden.

Excerpt from a Letter to my Associate Producer, Dyson Lovell, January 1975:

Nazareth: I see it made of white, dusty streets, poor houses with whitewashed walls, straw roofs, crowded around a square where meetings take place, exchanges, some little commerce, and in which a synagogue fronts, no poorer than the houses but hospitable as a home.

To find a village that could be Nazareth as I imagine it and have envisioned it is the prime and sole purpose of my on-the-spot investigations, and most important.

You must understand my problem: if I succeed in giving a credible, a true, image of that social and human dimension in which a mysterious design has placed the story of Jesus, I will have established the basis of a dramatic structure certainly closer to reality than to legend. Nazareth will be the touchstone of the Hebraic world, the meeting point of religious ideas current at the time of Christ, and above all the field where the seeds of the messianic expectation sown over centuries by the prophets have succeeded by now in ripening the fruits of hope and, at the same time, a feverish anxiety.

I count on good luck and my stubbornness. It would sicken me to have to build a papier-mâché Nazareth, to set out on my journey toward the Gospels from Cinecittà station.

Excerpt from a Letter to Vincenzo Labella, our producer, Fez, Morocco,

April 20, 1975:

With Renzo and Gianni [Renzo Mongiardino and Gianni Quaranta, the two production designers of the film] we reached a decision yesterday: we will go to Volubilis, a Roman city, a survivor, partially, of earthquakes and destructions, and partly disinterred by loving and patient care.

We passed through the village of Moulay Idriss, a pilgrimage center. Here everything is an olive festival; Umbria and Galilee seem mirrored on these lovely hills, the same clear air, the same shades of green, the brown, ocher earth.

Beyond Moulay Idriss there is a crossroad: to the left you descend toward Volubilis, to the right you rise toward Fertassa. Ramdani, our

Moroccan guide, tells me that this is a tiny village, so poor that electricity has not arrived there yet. I had the strange sensation of having been there before! I said we should visit Volubilis later, but now let's go to Fertassa.

Dear Vincenzo, you can't know how I regret that you were not with us yesterday.

My dream, my plans, my hopes: everything was there. Unbelievable! Just the way I had designed it!

Some roofs have to be taken down, some walls restored. But everything is just right, all perfect, really. After two hours or more (time had gone by and now who knows when we will see Volubilis!) we moved about as though within my own Nazareth. Here's Mary's house, there's Joseph's, and the Rabbi Yehuda's; the square with the synagogue, and the well for water.

The people welcomed us right away with smiles and friendly gestures: we go into houses, into the tiny courtyards where the women bake bread and the men weave baskets. There are no beds, no furniture, no cupboards. Oil lamps are arranged in niches in the walls; the few garments are hung on pegs; one sleeps on straw mats.

The village is truly primitive, but the people who live here are happy. Fertassa looks out over a stupendous plain, like the valley below Assisi. Its rear is protected by the mountain and by the holy Moulay Idriss.

It still has the same fountain that gave water to the Roman soldiers of Volubilis. Women carry water jars on their heads, such as I've seen in Galilee; children are barefoot, like flocks of sparrows.

I know that the production will have logistical problems of every kind to contend with. But this *is* Nazareth. A miracle too beautiful, which convinces me to insist on Fertassa as a nonnegotiable condition for realizing the film!

CHAPTER 3

From Morocco to Tunisia

The following scenes I had decided to shoot in Morocco: the Magi, the Herodian scenes, many of the main sermons of Jesus, including the Sermon on the Mount, the multiplication of the loaves, and a number of others.

Then we moved to Tunisia, with its glorious, ever-changing scenery. There, as I have said, our people were building the Temple, which, once we had finished shooting the scenes of Jerusalem, had to be transformed for the interiors of Pilate. At the same time we were re-creating the great square of Jerusalem in the Monastir fort. Other related scenes were to be shot between Monastir and Sousse, a city farther up the coast toward Tunis.

We were fortunate in finding, along this coast, spacious living quarters providing comfortable lodgings for the actors, extras, and technicians. At Sousse I decided to shoot Golgotha and the exterior scenes of Jerusalem as well as many of the interiors, such as the house of Elizabeth and the synagogue of Bethlehem. Finally, in the environs of Sousse at a place called Latma, we created a small lake and built a wharf to simulate the landing place for the fishermen at Capernaum.

The location search lasted all of 1974 and was protracted into the summer of 1975. Immediately afterward, the labor of reconstruction began and was entrusted to a marvelous group of Italian technicians and artists with prodigious skills.

Our constructions were so imposing and spectacular that tourists in Tunisia began to come in large groups to visit and admire them. Their enthusiasm inspired the municipality of Monastir to set up a regular tourist itinerary with the "Temple" an obligatory stop.

In no time, the astute local vendors invaded the place selling the tourists souvenirs of their "new Temple"!

When our work was over, the Tunisian government refused our offer to demolish the buildings, which instead are now preserved at no little cost so as not to deprive Monastir of a prime tourist attraction.

Random Notes from the Location Search:

Tunisia, July 1975

We are crossing Chott Djerid, or the Great Salt Desert, and are beginning to know absolute heat—heat that transforms the terrain into a furnace, obliterates every trace of vegetation, suspends mirages between earth and heaven. Some hope of being able to arrive and drink that water shimmering on the horizon—a lake, a river, a sea that does not exist, except as a cruel joke this implacable sun plays on the earth.

As my cameraman was physically melting, he gasped:

"Just the place to send the family for summer holidays!"

Tozeur is a city of strange geometry and even stranger architecture decorated with bricks ranged in most fanciful patterns.

The horrible afternoon heat drove us into an alley, and then into the blue and white coolness of a courtyard upon which opened the rooms of a house inhabited by women and children. They are the custodians of a tomb of a saint of Islam who sleeps there, near their cots, in a tomb decorated with ribbons and flags of all colors.

The women weave rugs. They are lost behind designs that repeat themselves like sets of Chinese boxes. The young girls are dancing about, occupied with their child's play; the bigger ones hide themselves behind the columns of the portico that surround the courtyard: they wink, their wily eyes are laughing, they shy away until they see the cameras pointed at them, then they make a rapid gesture, rubbing their fingers to suggest an offering of some dinar before allowing us to photograph them.

Not far from them a blind camel heads its endless path to raise the water from a well.

There are no votive offerings, no souvenirs or little pictures, in this domestic sanctuary. The cheerfulness of the children, the swift, ceaseless labor of the mothers, give rise to a strange peace, mixed with quick smiles and the pungent odor of couscous cooking.

Nefta is a large village at the edge of the Sahara. The sands press against its walls, whirled by the wind. Palm trees, protected too, very tall, thin palm trees such as I have never seen before. For a moment, I thought I might be able to make this my Bethlehem, but the memory of Tinerhip suppressed this thought. The Moroccan city is more alive, better for accentuating the contrast between the poverty of the birth of Jesus and the festive atmosphere of the city, a city unaware of the tiny drama that has for protagonists a carpenter from Nazareth and his young wife.

Castled at the top of a peak, Temezreth in Tunisia dominates the valley of Matmata, where the inhabitants live underground to escape the heat and the sandstorms, a strange place, infinitely stimulating for the creative imagination.

Temezreth is entirely built with stones and was suggested to me as an alternative for Nazareth. I refused it at once, but the place enchanted me.

The homes, all of them, have gardens and courtyards where the wind snaps, and flaps the clothes hung out to dry like ships' sails. Perhaps for this reason, the air smacks of the sea.

I thought of locating Capernaum here. But the only mountain road leading to it is impracticable for large vehicles. In the spring, with its great rains, it disappears immediately. How could we bring the boats here?! And then, there are no hotels.

Nannuzzi, our cameraman, is not losing his enthusiasm, and proposes that for the two weeks we have left we sleep here in tents, or in the underground houses of Matmata. He says that with a little spaghetti and a guitar, it wouldn't be so bad, and could even be fun.

There's no restaurant at Temezreth. We wind up satisfying our appetite and quenching our thirst with some excellent melons, under the kind shade of a few trees lost like a patrol in the middle of the desert.

It was at Temezreth that I assisted at a Berber wedding, which is like others I have seen in Israel, in the Sinai, and in Jordan.

A letter of April 26, 1975 to Vincenzo Labella from Marrakech:

I am writing to you aboard a Pullman as we leave Marrakech. As we traveled toward the mountain passes of the Atlas, the red walls of the city behind us seemed aflame. We passed villages, sites, hills with castles of straw and mud, others like fortresses and as ponderous as the architecture of Sangallo, despite the fragility of the material with which they are built. But still nothing like Nazareth. The olive groves here are sparse and the land scorched.

But then, I found at Tinghir and Ouarzazate the backgrounds and ideal locations for all the episodes of Herod, with the census, and the slaughter of the innocents, and most important of all, the location for Bethlehem.

Around the square of Tinghir there are houses almost bizarre in appearance and color. A series of endless arches enclose the area, adding a surprisingly dynamic force to the view. Here I envisage the arrival of Mary and Joseph, alone, bewildered, in the hubbub of a city in festival.

Here, in this same square, I see the total desolation that follows the slaughter ordered by Herod. The wind blows freely. It lifts the dust and makes the gates and doors of the houses and shops whine.

With Nannuzzi, I have already studied some shooting angles. But I warn you that the deadly job here will be in production. The site is covered with an unbelievable layer of filth, and it will take weeks, and many trucks, to clean the square to guarantee a minimum of hygiene. But this is Bethlehem, and Herod lives a short distance away, at Ouarzazate, a menacing and sumptuous Machaerus, where we will also set the episode of Herod Antipas, Herodias, and Salome and the first encounter with John the Baptist.

Meanwhile, wardrobe is discovering mines of props: furniture, weapons, costumes, rugs, and tapestries, which the Moroccan artisans, mostly Berbers, are producing or will produce expressly for us.

In these handmade objects, the very soul of these marvelous people is expressed—through their traditions and through the genius that shows itself in their songs, in their music, in their dance.

We are now in the north, in the actual city of Meknes, resplendent with palaces and mosques. Coming down from Erfur, we have seen, not far from Azrou, the perfect place for the Nativity: a natural grotto, which one approaches up a slight incline.

(We will have to think in good time about the Newborn, which we must entrust to our Mary.)

CHAPTER 4

So Many Stars, But Only One Star

It didn't take long for a somewhat clamorous publicity to develop around the film. It was in those fatuous tones that some of the press assume particularly when facing matters out of the ordinary. But most of it concentrated on the fact that the cast that had been gathered was made up of many of the most famous names in the cinema's Who's Who.

Most smiled, and said it was a Cecil B. De Mille operation with all the bass drum and fanfare to open up a parade of movie stars on the posters.

How wrong they were.

None of the artists had been chosen because of a recognized name or for his or her renown but only, and exclusively, because we wanted the best choice, the best casting for each role, however small.

Further, I must emphasize something about the extraordinary participation of celebrities in the film. Everyone, without exception, accepted fees far below their due. We made it clear to everyone. "The only star of this project is the Star of Bethlehem. We are all at his service. We cannot allow ourselves to pay the figure that each one personally deserves." And they all waived their legitimate salaries for the experience of taking part in an undertaking so different —and under such a lofty sign!

I must add that the rock that started the avalanche was the commitment of Laurence Olivier. He accepted our invitation to play the part of Nicodemus, most of all because of his Christian faith, and also because of our firm and long-standing friendship.

After his decision, many others came with warm enthusiasm and a spirit of collaboration that went far beyond their professional obligation. I renewed old acquaintances and generated new friendships, for which I am eternally grateful.

That these great artists chose *Jesus,* turning down more lucrative offers and less demanding work seemed to me another verification of that "conspiracy of events." For example, I happened to mention: "Of course, the ideal Magdalene would be Anne Bancroft." I remembered her as superb, from *Anne of the Miracles* to *The Graduate,* but realized I was asking the impossible. She is an actress who works seldom—by choice. She doesn't like to be away from her home with husband, Mel Brooks, and her children. She demands prohibitive fees mainly to discourage requests and remain at peace.

Three days later they called me from London: Anne Bancroft has accepted!

I thought Mastroianni would be fine as Pilate, but he wasn't available. The only other person I felt could be right was Rod Steiger. A week doesn't pass and Steiger telegraphs: "Most happy to participate in your film." Almost every great actor has dreamed of interpreting Pilate. And Miss Bancroft told me that she had always been fascinated by the figure of Mary Magdalene. She once described her thoughts about her acceptance of the part:

"I chanced to receive an offer from a director I respected that I couldn't refuse—a project that gives me every guarantee, surrounded by companions I admire totally. There's little money, but never mind. I can earn more in other projects less exciting than this one, which at least will give me satisfaction in playing the role."

And so for Rod Steiger, who immediately said when he arrived: "I do it, I do it—and don't ask me how much I want."

Anthony Quinn as Caiaphas, Rascel for the man born blind, Ernest Borgnine for the Centurion, and many others accepted with the same enthusiasm.

I do not pretend to assume a privileged position, but I firmly believe that all of us, in one way or another, are called to take upon ourselves a responsibility, an initiative, to perform a deed, accomplish an undertaking—in short, to become instruments of God.

For me, I had at my disposal an exceptional group of artists. It would have been unreasonable and absurd not to involve them in my project only because they were well known. Their fame is not only authenticated through the chemistries of publicity but is born from a serious professionalism. So many key personalities that crowd the story of Jesus are very complex. To leave them to the interpretative abilities of unknown actors or simply nonprofessionals, as many directors have done, would have seemed to me to contradict a fundamental understanding of dramatic presentation. The most difficult parts of a musical score are entrusted only to a soloist. Why should it be otherwise for a performance in a film?

It is true that at times the casting of new names and faces has had happy results. But the bigger the undertaking, the more necessary it is to reduce to a minimum the risk of failing with unproven choices. I faced the task of directing six or more hours of film, in other words, three films of two hours in one project: a film destined for half a billion spectators, to be launched on the threshold of spring. The shooting schedule was regulated like a watch, with time cut to a minimum. The working plan had to be continually juggled and revised to co-ordinate the dates the various actors were available and not overload the operation with unnecessary expense, but above all, to avoid the horror of going beyond the contracted finishing dates. Therefore I considered it essential for the well-being and success of the film that it be firmly anchored with artists of proven talent, professionals whose presence would be a stimulus to do better and, most important, a protection against that "decline of tone" that is inevitable when polished actors must play against those less accomplished.

Here is Olivier repeating the prophecy of Isaiah surrounded by the sorrowful imagery of the sheep brought to the shearer. It stands silently, like the servant of God who, though scorned and hurt, beaten and wounded, doesn't let a complaint pass his lips. With his rich talent he reached the peak of authentic inspiration.

And he achieved this result without virtuoso showiness but simply as if he had been preparing for the part, not for months, but for years. The words of the prophet issued from his lips in a whisper. They were not recited, but seemed, rather, born in him as an exact echo of the sacrifice that was unfolding before his eyes of the innocent, the just, the Son of God, mounted on the cross amidst the mourning and wailing of a troubled people.

With Olivier there was no need to discuss how to re-create the emotion of that moment, or of those words. Nor did we discuss, but only read together, the beautiful scene of the meeting between Nicodemus and Jesus when he invites Nicodemus "to be born again."

There is that capacity in Olivier to suffuse himself with light. He gives the spectator the distinct impression of radiance, convincing one of the reality of the human drama that he is going through as a Jew of the ancient faith. He sees the prophecy fulfill itself before his eyes. Too late, with the sacrifice concluded, he understands Jesus to be the true Messiah—God, who takes upon himself all the sins of the world and heals the wounds of mankind then gives it rebirth.

But how can one do justice to all the actors who put their hearts and the fruit of years of experience and sacrifice into this film?

Did they do it merely to add a pearl, great or small, to the crown of their successes?

I do not believe it. I have to say that I am ever more strongly and clearly convinced that even the most prejudiced of them, those who perhaps had lent their names to the film with far different goals and purposes—even they found themselves trapped in a "conspiracy of events" not unlike that which brought me on my own "road to Damascus."

Really, much of this film was a paradise on earth visited from time to time by Spirits in a state of grace.

I remember the evenings after the long days of work. We would gather together in the simple but comfortable living quarters. We would sit around a table or on the floor. These nights made us feel as if we had been taken "by magic and put into a jar" to rediscover the ideal of friendship with a feel of festivity that the many busy days in the past had denied us.

What a rare "school" this film *Jesus* was for that strong group of young actors, whether apostles or small-part players of our "repertory factotum," working and living side by side with the greatest talents of the cinema and world theater. They saw transformed before their eyes the frantic John the Baptist of Michael York, tawny as a desert lion; the Herod of Peter Ustinov, such a prodigious medley of grotesque and barbaric ferocity; the Joseph of Arimathea of James Mason, a model of style and charm; the Herod Antipas of Christopher Plummer, everything played on chords of uncertainty befitting a man tempted by the voice of justice but too corrupt to be able to respond to it. And the Barabbas of Keach, who gives powerful voice to all the liberation instincts of rebellion for all time, yet blinded by his own political myopia, is generous to the point of risking his life in open struggle against the oppressor.

What lessons for the young actresses in following the refined, subtle touches of the Herodias of Valentina Cortese or the emotional intensity of our other four actresses, Regina Bianchi, Marina Berti, Maria Carta, and Claudia Cardinale.

An extraordinarily rich gallery to which I will never tire of returning, in memory and in heart, under the sign of that Star that surely guided us all.

CHAPTER 5

Jesus and Rome

From the moment I finally decided to do the film, my life became a succession of happy experiences. In the first place, as I have said, there was the rediscovery of the Gospel, a unique occasion for anybody, especially for someone of mature years. And then, the possibility of visiting the Mediterranean and the countries that border it, places I did not really know, though I had traveled extensively in northern Europe and America.

I retraced Jesus' path with the discomforting realization that very few of the places would still be intact. It was almost like hoping to find untouched corners of Rome from the time of Caesar or Marcus Aurelius in the Rome of today. Some columns, some ruins remain, to give witness here and there, but the life, the day-in-and-day-out flavor, is buried beneath strata of successive civilizations. The character, the original spirit, of Judea and of Palestine, has been lost, just as that kind of community from which Jesus emerged has been almost entirely lost. Golgotha itself, which was located outside of the gate of Damascus between the first and the second circle of walls, is now buried under buildings. There were four hundred steps, no more, from the Tower of Antonius to the place of execution, not even three-hundred meters. And the sepulcher is nearby. As in all of the ancient world, the place of execution was located at the main gate of the city, right on the street where there was most traffic. The uprights of the beams were permanent, as a warning to visitors and to foreigners to note the efficiency of justice, swift to punish criminals with a horrible death. In plain view at the top of every cross the crime was written: "Thief," "Adulterer," "Blasphemer," "Assassin," or as in the case of Jesus, the specific accusation, "King of the Jews," the accusation for which he was condemned and executed.

For the Romans it was an exact and pertinent statement, not an act of scorn as the Hebrews suspected. Jesus had been proclaimed Messiah and had been acclaimed by the approving crowd, on Palm Sunday, the son of David and the king of the Jews, and this took on a precise juridical meaning from the point of view of the Romans. For them, according to the *lex Julia maiestatis,* whoever abrogated to himself royal titles or powers of govement without the approbation of the emperor and of the Senate of Rome deserved death. Actually, if for the Romans it was a crime of high treason and for the Sanhedrin a sacrilege, for the people it was a deluded hope of obtaining from Christ a new status for their nation.

They had imagined this "liberator" to be a sort of new Solomon,

a new David, able to lift up again the people of Israel, to restore Israel to its dignity and its lost liberties and break free from the bondage of Rome.

With his arrival, that era of peace and harmony promised by the prophets of Israel would at last be inaugurated.

Instead, Jesus disappointed everybody. The new Jerusalem, he said, is not what you believe it to be. It is not the twelve tribes of Israel that count, but the peoples of all the world. They saw him deal with the Romans in the same way he dealt with Jews. How was such free and easy conduct possible for a Hebrew Messiah? He made it very clear by preaching that everybody was invited to the table of his Father: Pharisees, pagans, Romans, Jews . . .

A false Messiah, therefore, was held accountable for disillusioning and destroying hopes so eagerly cultivated. We can well imagine

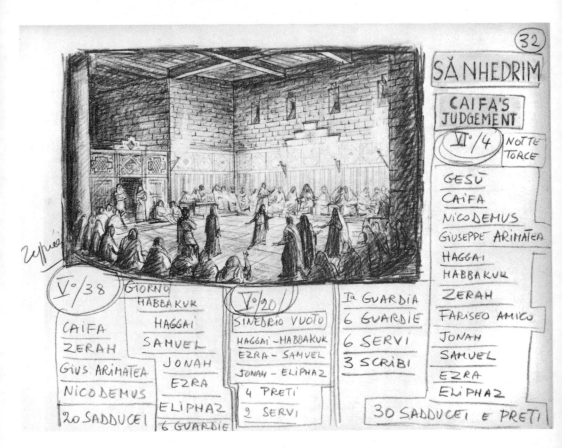

how the humiliation and ridicule from the Romans, brought about by Jesus, would weigh so heavily on the people of Jerusalem. And this explains the sudden movements, the enthusiastic reaction for Barabbas, the "famous patriot, arrested for sedition and homicide." Pilate offered the people a choice between the scorned, tortured Jesus, symbol of national humiliation, and the rebel Barabbas. He was well aware that the loudest and most decisive voices would be raised for Barabbas.

I would have wished, in the film, to give particular attention to the attitude of Rome in confronting the Jewish people and the Palestine of Jesus' time.

In fact, my scenario had included an opening sequence in the palace of Augustus at Rome and emphasized the aloofness with which the emperor regarded that remote corner of the empire. It was inhabited by a riotous, intractable people, divided by internal dissent, and ruled by Herod the Great, a monarch half-Hebrew but totally dedicated to Rome and to Caesar.

Often, bloody carnage followed attempts to force the Jews into recognizing and honoring the emperor's divinity, attempts such as that of Pompey (and later of Varus), who crushed the revolt of Judas the Galilean and the priest Zadok and crucified two thousand rebels. Rome finally relented and exempted the Hebrews from honoring the empreror's divinity and from military service in the armies of Rome, because conscription would automatically imply acceptance of the divine cult rendered to Caesar by his legions. The Jews were the only conquered people in the entire empire that were granted this exemption.

The film was already exceeding the most generous time limits. I had to abandon my plan to shoot that sequence and another, too, in which Augustus, on his deathbed, transferred the imperial power to the man who was to succeed him, Tiberius.

This was a painful sacrifice, and I deeply regretted not being able to fully delineate the context of the Roman world in confrontation with the Hebrew. It was a critical factor both for understanding the immense importance of Roman intervention with this troublemaker, Jesus, and for giving to the Gospel narrative (considered by some to be concerned more with doctrine than with actual history) incontrovertible historical support from the history of Rome, that which we know intimately and in a wealth of detail.

Still, in my film, imperial Rome is ominously present—even

apart from the discourses and the people's constant lamentations over the loss of liberty and the burden of fiscal oppression. An instance of this is found in the brief episode in which some mounted soldiers of a Roman squadron descend upon Nazareth at the very moment the twelve-year-old Jesus is being ceremonially inducted into the adult community of the synagogue.

I did not want to give this callous raid by Roman soldiers too violent or vicious a tone. I wanted, rather, to show how, in the face of Roman arrogance—ruthlessly snatching family provisions and the very bread of the Nazarenes, and laughing at their angry reaction—the people's sense of humiliation was inversely proportionate to the insults and scorn they received. Death at the hand of the oppressor is often suffused with an aura of heroism—infinitely

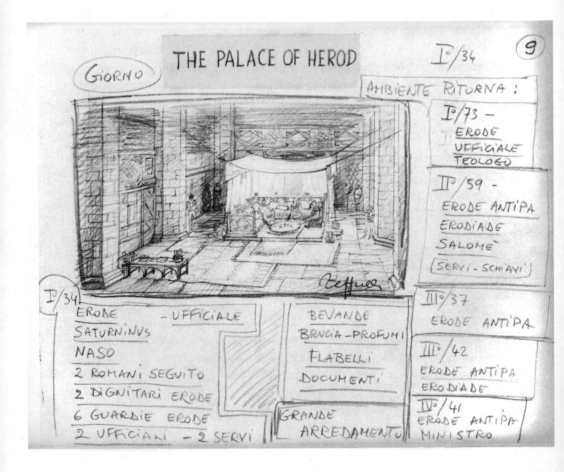

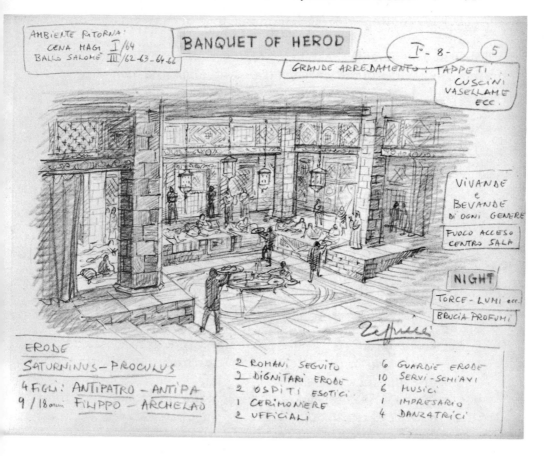

preferable to derision and scorn that grind into the ground the last shreds of one's self-respect.

Yet, in the final phases of the story of Jesus, Rome is there in all its majesty and juridical severity.

Now it is the procurator Pontius Pilate who must restrain the Jews' desire for revenge. Pilate was a career functionary with some military achievements to his credit, but he lacked necessary political acumen. He caused serious difficulties for himself in Rome by some mindless decisions and clearly criminal acts, such as trying to force veneration of the statue of Tiberius by ordering some soldiers to enter the Temple and mix with the worshipers. At a signal, three soldiers suddenly drew their daggers from under their capes and went wild in swift and brutal slaughter.

Anxious to remain in Caesar's favor and to keep his post, Pilate must have confronted Jesus determined to avoid any possible provocation.

Totally ignorant of that preacher's mission and quite unaware of the complexities of the Jewish religious situation, the Roman governor could have had only two considerations in mind:

One, Jesus is a popular figure, able to captivate the crowd with his charismatic personality and words. He is capable, therefore, of repeating and aggravating the upheavals already decried by the leaders of the Sanhedrin, which were no doubt observed with interest by Roman officials.

Two, the Sanhedrin leadership, for reasons of religious orthodoxy and political prudence, considers Jesus dangerous, and they report him to Roman authorities as a threat not only to peace of conscience but to civil order.

To ignore this report would be to expose oneself to possible recrimination that could then reach the emperor himself.

I am convinced that the convergence of these two attitudes, the Sanhedrin's, which rejects the Nazarene as a blasphemer, and Pilate's, which in the end considers him a very serious risk, sealed the condemnation of Jesus—a Roman condemnation, nonetheless.

For the first time in the history of films or plays about the life of Christ, the Roman procurator is seen and heard pronouncing the ritual sentence of crucifixion, a sentence we have examples of in the records of the court trials of the first martyrs.

When I discussed with Rod Steiger the attitudes of the character of Pilate, I saw at once that this intelligent "method" actor had prepared himself well by drawing upon every possible historical source that might throw light upon that complex character.

Frankly, given his reputation for an almost neurotic meticulousness—acquired probably during his formative years with the Actors Studio—I was afraid that I would have a very difficult time with Steiger. In fact, he arrived with clear ideas on how to address and resolve every aspect, every stop and comma, of his role.

Nothing bad about that, of course. The danger, I thought, was rather in his tendency to burden the character of Pilate with too profound an awareness of the "historical" importance of his meeting with Jesus. Pilate, in fact, could not possibly have known that he was co-protagonist in one of the greatest turning points in history.

I congratulated him on his professionalism, his dedication, and on the love with which he embraced this part. And then I told him

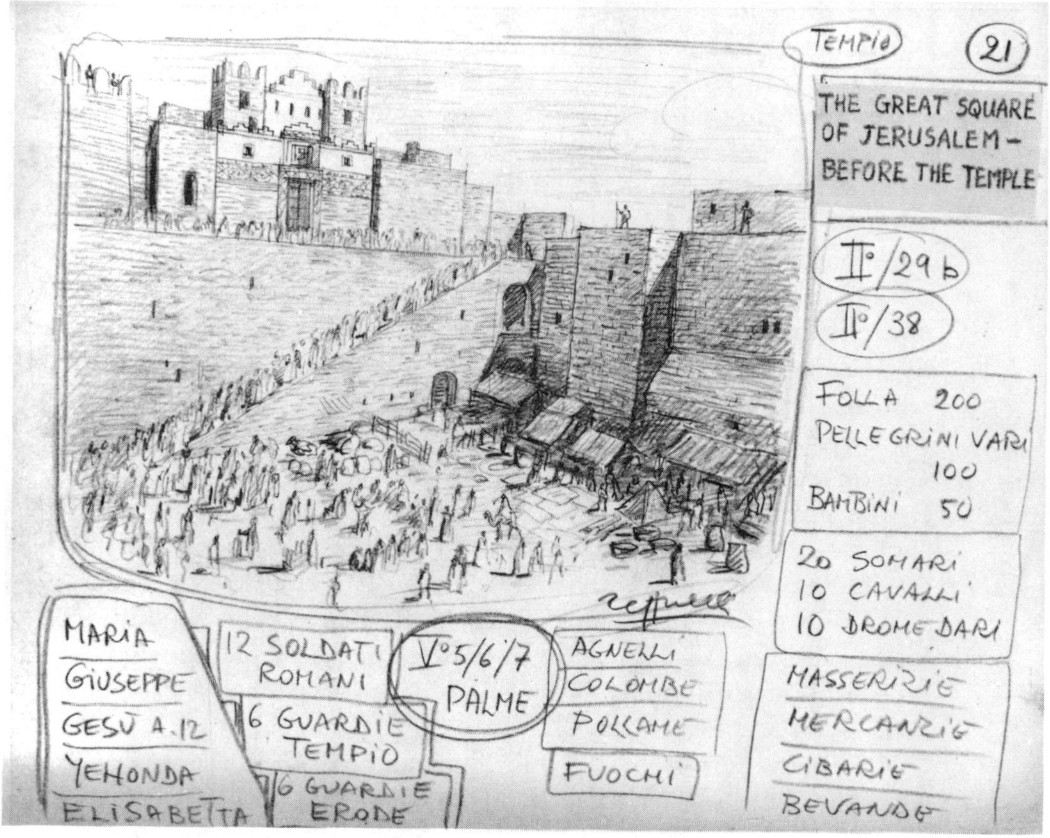
TEMPIO
21
THE GREAT SQUARE OF JERUSALEM - BEFORE THE TEMPLE
II°/29 b
II°/38
FOLLA 200
PELLEGRINI VARI 100
BAMBINI 50
20 SOMARI
10 CAVALLI
10 DROMEDARI
MARIA
GIUSEPPE
GESÙ A.12
YEHONDA
ELISABETTA
12 SOLDATI ROMANI
6 GUARDIE TEMPIO
6 GUARDIE ERODE
V°5/6/7
PALME
AGNELLI
COLOMBE
POLLAME
FUOCHI
MASSERIZIE
MERCANZIE
CIBARIE
BEVANDE

my fears and asked him to read Anatole France's intriguing short story in which Pilate, a frustrated and disenchanted exile in Marseille, is approached by someone who asks him about the trial of a certain Galilean prophet over which he had presided long ago when he was governor in Jerusalem. Hopelessly, the aging Pilate tries to remember the case; his memory is blank. And, as I recall, he winds up by saying something like this: "If I can't remember it, that means it wasn't important. It must have been one of those fanatics I sent to the cross."

Pilate's complete oblivion enlightened Steiger immediately, and he took advantage of it masterfully when his casual unconcern in his meetings with Jesus—conducted as a routine official chore—collapses with the uneasiness that Jesus arouses in him.

Here Steiger, with superb artistry, was able to bring into focus two or three moments of confusion experienced by that frontier functionary when illumined by a ray of light he could not comprehend but that he felt through the inmost fibers of his being.

So much so that, before pronouncing Jesus' condemnation, his final words spoken to an aide who urges him to ponder the risk he takes in freeing Barabbas (a known enemy of Rome), are these: "I ask myself who is the real enemy?" And his helpless glance searches the bloody visage of Jesus.

In murmuring those brief words, Steiger was able to flash across our minds the whole history of the coming clash between Christianity and the empire, out of which Rome would emerge battered but reborn.

A very special figure in the Roman occupation is the Centurion —in this film believably and honestly portrayed by Ernest Borgnine. He had become so "Roman" that he spent much of his time between shots talking and joking with the grips, the authentic Romans, resembling them physically, talking and gesticulating like them.

Contrary to what one might expect, Roman soldiers on duty in Judea were few, slightly more than three or four squadrons quartered in Caesarea, and only in emergencies reinforced by legions from Syria and Egypt.

We know which legions and how many were in Syria at this time, the Third Galilean and the Tenth Feratan, and in Egypt, the Third Cyrenian and the Twelfth Deiatorian. But fear not! The film spares you this lesson in Roman military history!

The Roman troops occupying Palestine were recruited from all around the empire. The fierce torture of the crown of thorns following the flagellation is directly linked to a typical game of Syrian soldiers.

Given the rather minimal presence of the Roman military in Judea, a centurion was a noncommissioned officer of much prestige in the public eye. For that reason the official's act of faith when he asked Jesus to heal his servant had to appear all the more remarkable.

History records an episode (the original script includes it) that honors the Jewish people and witnesses to their resistance to the Roman occupation. Their defiance of Pilate was shown by a delegation of Jews presenting themselves before him at Caesarea and standing motionless, offering their breasts and necks to the swords of the legionnaires to force the procurator to exempt their people from the obligation of venerating Caesar as divine.

The spiritual lymph vivifying every Jew, and derived directly from the Scriptures, formed the spine of a nation that has come through the centuries with its tradition and rites intact and, most of all, with the patrimony of its Law inviolate.

In Jerusalem, in Morocco, and in Tunisia I visited Jews who could be said to have walked out of the pages of Exodus: a people removed in time from the ancient prophets but near to them by the constancy of their faith in the one God of Israel and in the endurance of this Law.

Notes of a Journey:

Tunisia, July 1975

On the Island of Djerba I visited the "Hebrew patriarchs": a group of old men who frequent the synagogues (the oldest in North Africa). You find them seated by the sacred edifice, bronzed by the sun and made solemn as statues by their great white beards that stand out against their

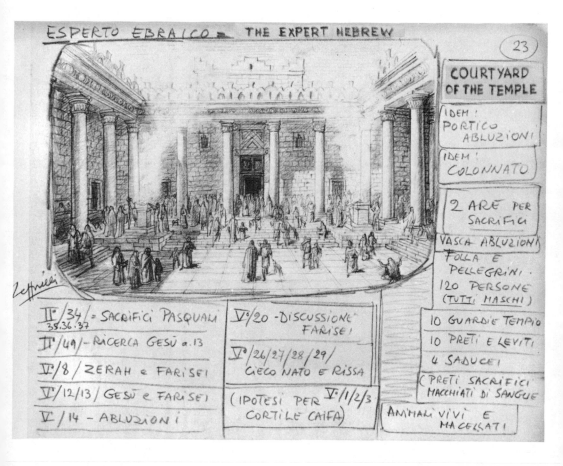

darkened skin. I met the leader of this thousand-year-old community and asked if he would be agreeable to having the "patriarchs" take part in some of the synagogue scenes. The old men listen to our discussions dispassionately, observing with innocent eyes our concern as image-hunters. One of them smiled and told the others, in Hebrew, what we were asking. The idea of a trip to the mainland delighted them. Laughing in the sun they were like children who had been promised a holiday. The prophets must have looked just like them—and like those the people of Jesus called Rabbi.

CHAPTER 6

Happiness on Earth

I have said that I was concerned about infusing into the script, to some degree at least, that vital quality of emotional openness and sensitivity that allows a too-often discussed matter to come alive again.

I wanted to know, to inform myself, to understand and to be enlightened, but not to the point of becoming a slave to data. It is far more rewarding to sense certain things and then reconstruct them as the fruit of the imagination than to draw a detailed blueprint of your ideas.

In the Gospels one can find what suits one's purpose. The scope is limitless, so much so that you can always advise an unhappy person to read the Gospels. In those pages you will find your answer, always.

Those answers, of course, are demanding, because at the opening of every discourse in the Gospels there is the usual terrifying question: Do you or do you not believe that you are part of God? If the answer is yes, anything that is against God will not do, and it must be rejected. A reading of the Gospels helps you emerge from the animal state in which you are immersed and assists you in attaining your greatest dignity. With this dignity you can free yourself from anything, from every chain, from all meanness—even that of so-called social progress, to which all of us are slaves. This foolish slavery poses a serious problem.

All of us—the young, particularly, who are most vulnerable, who pass hours and hours in the lap of consumerism, who grow drunk on it—we all betray our high destiny and at the same time we create another one, a tragic one, precisely with this encumbrance of things, of possessions, of objects: the fear of death. Because, when you come down to it, all this material comfort that surrounds us leaves us unprepared for the only question that matters, the great dilemma of life and death. At this juncture they are rich who are most prepared, the unprepared are the impoverished. It is customary to take literally, for example, the words of Jesus to the rich young man—"Leave everything and follow me"—and to take them as a socialist discourse. In fact, the Marxist error of seeing Jesus as a socialist is based on this text.

Socialism means an equal division of the goods of this earth, and that would be fine if it made room also for our supernatural destiny. Instead, it doesn't even consider it, and offers us no answer to our most disquieting questions. I believe, rather, that Jesus wanted us to understand something very important: everything that binds you to earth alienates you from God. If, through some special gift, you succeed in overcoming the obstacle of riches and "fortune" (haven't there been, possibly, saintly kings?) and in preserving an attitude of love toward humanity and God, then you, too, can attain the highest and most important goal.

But it seems to me that Jesus also says something more on this matter. Here especially, during my study for the film, a great window of hope, as it were, opened up for me, a vista of which I was unaware and that few, I believe, have focused on sufficiently. With regard to the renunciation of possessions and earthly bondage, Jesus not only promises a reward after death but guarantees it to us here on earth while we are still alive! His Kingdom brings it to us while we are still living, because earth should not be a planet of sorrow and renunciation, but of joy, of sweet sleep and peaceful days. And it is, in fact, by freeing ourselves from the slavery of the endless oppressions of matter that we will become just, tranquil, at peace.

CHAPTER 7

The Film Scenario

By May 1974 the first draft of the scenario was completed. For this task, we had commissioned Anthony Burgess, a man of delicate sensibilities and a phenomenal command of the English language—along with that, a man utterly fascinating because of the uncommon cast of his mind and his prodigious memory. He reminded me of the celebrated Pico della Mirandola. When Burgess reads a page, it sinks in and roots itself in his mind and metabolizes immediately as a catalyst for his latent ideas.

He was an agnostic, then converted to the Catholic faith. His was a mature and positive choice, not passive or casual. If you consider that he was already one of the most discerning novelists of our age, among the most prominent Shakespearean experts, a talented musician too, then, with his collaboration in the television script for *Moses,* you will easily understand why I considered him the obvious choice for this difficult task.

In only sixteen days he sketched a skeletal story of six acts. He made no reference to any literary source relating to Jesus. He had only to resort to the library of his memory, to materials sifted and retained from his previous readings.

The result was a draft profoundly permeated with the tone and meaning of the Gospel narrative, but often the dialogue of the various characters did not fit the Gospel records, especially in the words Burgess wanted to ascribe to Jesus.

As I was determined to make this film rigorously didactic, unfortunately, a conflict arose between my aims and the historical, theological, and mystical reworking of the Gospels that Burgess had prepared.

But the most severe confrontation that Burgess had to face was with a group of scriptural experts that the company had put at our disposal, recognizing a reasonable need for comfort and assurance in matters where I needed advice so as to avoid errors, inaccuracies, and perhaps some unevenness. These scholars had an easy game in criticizing the Gospel potpourri that Burgess had put together. They rejected countless points with the punctilious ardor in which one might defend one's own knowledge against another's errors—especially as regards words attributed to Jesus, inimitable words, irreplaceable, quite final.

I found myself unwittingly on the side of the scriptural experts; because I had planned to have all the characters of the Gospel panorama quite free to follow their own interpretations, open to the winds of fantasy, to the creative imagination of the actor—with due caution, of course.

But Jesus had to be interpreted otherwise, in the most orthodox way, with materials emerging from the Gospels themselves.

Unfortunately, Burgess, in his most interesting attempt to set the character of Jesus on a plane more accessible to us today, too freely put mere human words on his lips, a different language quite unsuited for the very purpose he wanted to achieve. Simply in having loved him so much, in having made him so much his own, Burgess ultimately destroyed the charismatic, mystical stature that for me sustained the character of Christ.

Even with an intensely human touch to Jesus, the man-god, a "presence" easily accessible to us, one cannot obscure the divine radiance that his person emanates at every moment. Everything, every act, every word of Jesus must disclose this double aspect. When Jesus put his hand on the shoulder of a friend, that gesture inevitably took on a sacred quality; when he broke the bread, when he patted the head of a child—ordinary activities, yes, but they assumed a unique character because his every gesture, his every word, exuded the power between God and himself and all earthly things.

This was always the most troubling issue to resolve in directing the character that the English actor Robert Powell had the impossible task of playing. And since an actor's art is such that its very existence relies on the use of merely human means and is, therefore, inevitably liable to fall back on so-called tricks of the trade, from the very beginning I chose a passive route. I kept the actor from resorting to certain easy interpretative solutions, hoping instead little by little that he would discover within himself that style, those solutions, that would be nearest to the most convincing representation of the "divine."

Since I firmly believe that every person, even the weakest and the vilest, contains within him a touch of the divine—a light that God has breathed into him—with Robert Powell, I succeeded in arousing and drawing forth from his personality that part of him that seemed for me to speak of things divine. The eyes, which, more than anything else of the human body, are the portals to the spirit, became in Powell two penetrating beams of light. His voice, which, not by chance, was called *the* word in our ancient language, took on mysterious and distant resonances in him, as though he were transmitting and evoking messages from unknown sources.

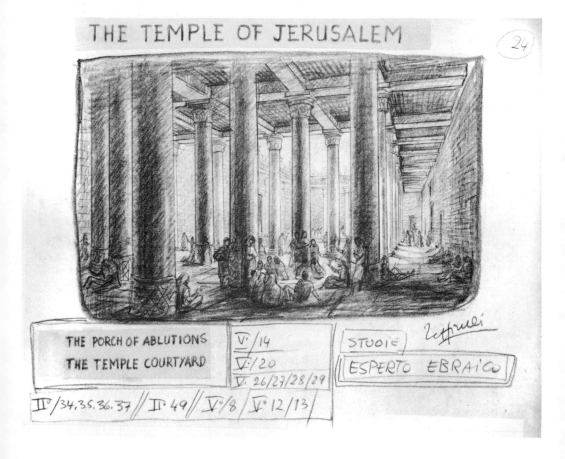

THE TEMPLE OF JERUSALEM

(24)

THE PORCH OF ABLUTIONS — V·/14 — STUOIE — Zeffirelli

THE TEMPLE COURTYARD — V·/20 — ESPERTO EBRAICO

V· 26/27/28/29

II°/34.35.36.37 // II· 49 // V·/8 / V· 12/13/

If this was the disturbing dilemma of every scene in which the character of Jesus appeared, the other aspect of directing this drama —the human, the everyday, visible and tangible for human senses, had to be kept constantly and equally under strict control.

There were points I remembered from recent and long-ago reading in the correspondence of Don Milani, a biblical scholar, with a French director, Maurice Cloche, who had approached him to ask for his collaboration in drafting a scenario for a film to be made on Christ. Don Milani, modest as always and aware of the responsibilities he bore as head of his exemplary community, politely declined the offer but did not hesitate to give the director some advice that he considered pertinent for one engaged in such a lofty theme.

He concentrated on the dual nature of the character of Jesus, man and God.

Strange, but today it is easier to believe in Jesus as God than Jesus as a man. The film must make exceedingly clear what exactly is meant by the words: "And the Word was made *flesh.*"

Scenes of Palestine (views, houses, streets, shops, works, domestic chores, *misery,* filth, etc.) will give a far more accurate understanding than a plethora of words.

To go and capture on film the hunger that haunts Palestine today will give us a more realistic setting for the life of our Lord. A nation of slaves, crowds without bread, babies with rickets, diseases of every kind (your own *Monsieur Vincent!*)—there it is, the world that Jesus embraced.

The unemployed and the laborers must come out of the cinema knowing that Jesus lived in a world as sad as theirs, and that he, as they, felt that social injustice was blasphemous, that he too battled for a better world.

It's up to you to decide whether it would be better to shoot it all in the first person (Jesus on camera), or whether you might allow alternatives. If the latter, I suggest, by way of example, the following scenes:

The boy Jesus at school.

Ten or twenty boys are seated on the ground. A spectator knows that one of them is He, but doesn't know which.

The same scene at the Jordan.

The Baptist points to the crowd. "Behold the Lamb of God . . ." All eyes turn to see the Christ, the King so yearned for. Finally, the camera focuses on that spot: nine or ten faces of surprised young pilgrims. Which one is He? No one knows, it's one of them, it doesn't matter, what matters for us is that there seems to be nothing special about the group the Baptist had singled out. Jesus is there, but so much a human being as to be indistinguishable from the others.

Again, the arrest scene.

The camera focuses on the twelve faces. If Judas hadn't promised to point out Jesus he wouldn't have been recognized (Mt. 26:48). But when Judas moves, the camera is already on him, peering into his eyes. (Jesus is once again the subject searching the faces of his unhappy friends in vain for some sign of repentence.)

These three scenes or others like them will keep the film from giving the impression that this invisible Jesus had flesh different from that of the other characters. But perhaps they won't be necessary and it will suffice to have all eyes turn to Jesus to convey the precise impression of his location, and with that the evidence that he has a body.

Actually, it may have been his determination to follow Milani's enlightening suggestions, that compelled Anthony Burgess (an Englishman, and as such, incapable of blithely ignoring the canons of logic, and of escaping certain tendencies of his people, specifically that of following to the letter advice about which they have been quite convinced) to try desperately, in any way at all, to make Jesus humanly believable. But since the playwright's art is only one factor in any cinemagraphic production, as important as it may be, the ongoing and critical phase of every production escaped him—the picture, light, and sound encompassing the dialogue, at times miraculously resolve problems that the script can only hint at. Certain liberties, which are apparently quite compatible with the written word, turn out to be unacceptable after they have been tested.

However, in those sixteen days of work, carried almost to the limits of human endurance, Burgess dashed off the story of Christ as he remembered it. And so he put an outline at our disposal, a framework that, though it might have been an easy target for the scholars, embodied, nevertheless, all the story lines I as director needed for the film.

Anthony Burgess often finds it difficult to collaborate with others, and quite unaccustomed to working with a director in the production of a film. He took leave of us long before work began, and for two years we heard nothing from him. During those two years I asked myself with mounting anxiety whether the final draft of the film, so remote now from the original version, might in the end be rejected by him. True, I had at my side Suso Cecchi d'Amico, a screenwriter of profound understanding and insight, renowned for her ability to remain faithful to the original conception of a project —a virtue possessed by few.

D'Amico's presence guaranteed faithfulness to the substance and to the spirit that had inspired us from the beginning. It was important to me to preserve the original concept out of respect for Burgess. After the film was done, we showed him the first print with bated breath, prepared at the last moment to hear him ask that his name be disassociated from the project. On the contrary, after a six-and-a-half-hour showing, Burgess emerged profoundly moved. He took the first sheet of paper he could find and dashed off a letter of appreciation that I cherish. All the doubts, the anguish, the uncertainties that had weighed on the heart of this enlightened man during the scripting of *Jesus* had vanished. Humbly, he declared his happiness in having had a hand in the work.

CHAPTER 8

What Was Jesus Like?

A curious mental inconsistency inclines us to think of Jesus as born and raised in the climate of "our" religion. Not only is this wrong, but it puts serious obstacles in the way of our understanding of Christ himself. Jesus was a Jew, probably a Pharisee (not a Zealot as some have insisted), immersed in the most Jewish practices and customs imaginable. The Christian religion came much later (a schism from Judaism), out of the faith and controversies of his followers.

As good Jews, they weren't the least bit concerned about sketching the physical appearance of the Master for posterity. There is never a "physical" description of any of the Gospel characters. For that matter, the personal features or appearance of individuals are never described in the literature of the Middle East. Greece began to record such things, and in the *Iliad* every hero is described and his physical features and characteristics noted. But among the Jews the human body was of interest only as a dwelling of the spirit— especially because of the ancient Mosaic prohibition against human images.

Far more mysterious is the lack of information about Christ's eighteen years between the dispute with the doctors in the Temple and the beginning of his preaching. But the very fact that no one took the trouble to speak of those eighteen years implies that nothing exceptional happened to him. They were years of interior growth, perhaps years of study and development of ideas.

The portrait of Jesus is, then, an image that we have, little by little, drawn for ourselves.

Everyone, in every age—writer or painter, believer or nonbeliever—has tried to reconstruct the figure of Jesus from the Gospel. The great skeptics, naturally, were only concerned with turning to ashes every word, every affirmation, about the figure of the Christ of the New Testament, blotting out his image, just as true believers of every age have tried to fit Jesus to their own sentiments, tastes, needs, and current mentality. One of the great lay students of the Gospel, Loisy, understood that the "liberal" Jesus, born of the religious aspirations and the positivist needs of the time, at the beginning of our century, in no way coincided with the historical Jesus.

Nor does the earliest Christian literature tell us anything about the historical Jesus. There, the "Lord" is not an individual but a personification of the church's transcendent origins. Such an interpretation forces one to believe that the early Christians were in no way victims of their imagination, or of deceits, since they never regarded Christ as a man of flesh and blood, but as a symbol.

However, the historian Charles Guignebert, in his book *Christ*, observes: How is it possible that

". . . an obscure *nabi,* seen dimly by us in the Synoptics, could be so swiftly transformed into that sublime and divine being who is the "Lord" of Paul?

So the Christ for many would not be a man, but the personification of a social movement. For others he would be nothing other than the god of the syncretistic and mystic Judaic sect of the Nazors which, a century before the birth of Christ, rendered worship to a divine Liberator, to a Savior. The name of Jesus would mean nothing but "Yahnoeh who saves," that is, "Savior."

Psychologically he was generous, optimistic, with clearly benevolent and compassionate dispositions, even though at times he showed himself not immune to bursts of anger. What especially strikes one about Christ is the abiding revolutionary spirit of his thought, revolutionary, yet suffused with resignation, an antimony resolved in the affirmation of the supreme law of Love, which confers a marvelous and most original feeling on his preaching and his doctrine.

Legends soon circulated that would have him ugly, emaciated, even aloof, and others that make him handsome, even blond, curly-haired, with a flowing beard and imperious eyes. Justin writes that Christ appeared without beauty, without glory. Remodeling him according to Isaiah, Irenaeus describes him as weak, unimpressive, even ugly. Clement of Alexandria says that "he was not physically attractive," to convince us that beauty didn't matter in a man such as he. Origen goes still further, saying that Jesus was small of stature, ungraceful, appearing to be a man of no account. Commodianus has him as a man of humble aspect, like a slave.

One very ancient tradition would even have him leprous, just as some sects claimed that the mother of Jesus was a whore, since only out of the greatest of sins, from the most impure flesh, could be born the one who would save the world. Nevertheless, a feeling of union of beauty with divinity was not only widespread but necessary for every faithful follower. And so this Jesus began to exhibit—above all else—dignity, recalling Psalm 41:3:

"You are the most beautiful of the sons of men, grace is diffused upon your lips." The advocates of ugliness little by little lost ground even though they had on their side Basil and Cyril of Alexandria, who held that Christ had been "the ugliest of the sons of men."

How, then would we go about selecting a human face to represent the Lord's divinity on that deceptive little screen that so often brightens our evenings at home?

I was open to any solution, even to considering as a possibility, up to a point, an actor such as Dustin Hoffman, who is certainly not the usual, traditional image of the Nazarene; this actor is squat, and has a large nose, irregular features, and dark hair. There was another actor whom we considered for the part, Al Pacino—a Byzantine face, trained talent, but unfortunately too closely identified with characters of recent American cinema.

Yes, there had to be a solution. Where was the face that was inspired, convincing, unexpected?

The problem had so many agonizing and dramatic facets. Naturally so. If you are a painter or sculptor you make your Jesus for yourself as you wish him to be, with pencil, paper, colors. You design and shape the face that you imagine. But a film director works with material already shaped and formed.

For me this person could only be a particularly accomplished and professional actor. I shoot directed takes on every level. I don't resort to those devices characteristic of many of my colleagues, like Pasolini and others, who use someone more or less corresponding to the character they have imagined but who has no acting experience. The end result is a desperate search for some way to correct deficiencies with cinematic tricks. They even saddle an amateur with the voice of a professional, a device that I have never found to be convincing. You see, one cannot bring off this transforming action of reassembling a person with elements other than those that formed him or her. With this attempt, the breath of truth inevitably is lost. It was imperative for me to find an actor—and I mean an in-depth actor—who could bring Jesus alive for the screen. You may well imagine the difficulty of the search. Actors of just the right age who had the appearance I envisaged and who were available in the English-speaking world of the cinema or theater were very few.

CHAPTER 9

Robert Powell

Most actors would consider the role of Jesus a peak that, once reached, would be difficult to descend. There would be the fear of remaining Jesus all their lives, of not being able to abandon such a "definitive" character and go on to other roles.

I had insisted to my producers that if a satisfactory "Christ" was not found, the contract would be automatically canceled. I didn't want to embark on an undertaking with the pivot missing, the very hinge of the film.

We had probed, scoured, and searched even the most remote corners of the American and English theater. Then that vast breeding ground for fine actors, England, finally gave us the right man in the person of Robert Powell.

Here was an actor I had already seen. He had enjoyed a resounding success in a comedy that played for two years with superb reviews. As a person he appeared a bit eccentric, a type quite opposite to one you would imagine fitted for the part of Christ. He was a cynic and, yes, somewhat eccentric but—I must say—a consummate professional.

Even so, at this point I was a long way from considering him right for Christ. To me, he seemed to be perfect for the part of Judas. We did a screen test, and ignoring that curly hair of his, and the long neck, I concentrated on his eyes.

In the cinema the eyes are everything. When you think of it, why do we have eyes? They are not only to see with but to allow others to see us. The eyes express as a guiding lamp the strength of one's own spirit and character. Powell's eyes were so impressive that

I casually suggested to the producer and other collaborators that it might be worth the trouble to test him for Jesus.

The proposal was received with not a little skepticism and sarcasm. One of them even said that to think of the same actor for two parts as opposite as the Devil and holy water showed an obvious lack of clear thinking on my part.

Finally Sir Lew Grade, up to now the most ardent supporter of the film and obviously concerned about the search for an actor-Jesus, gave me the authorization for the screen test.

Immediately we restructured the test for Powell as Jesus. With the makeup staff and photographer Armando Nannuzzi, we went unhesitatingly for the classical image of the Nazarene—long hair parted in the middle and a trimmed beard.

Slowly, as the screen test progressed, we all noticed that something remarkable was happening. There was a sense of a miracle, a kind of "message" and "a transportation of matter." An image seemed to take shape around this man as if he were a medium. Even more impressive was a kind of aura "not of his own" that was settling on him.

While we were waiting in silence to begin to shoot, one of the seamstresses, who had worked in films all her life, was giving the final touches to the woolen veil covering the actor's head. Armando was whispering orders to his assistants and making the final adjustments on his lighting with that loving and obstinate care that makes him unequaled at his art.

At a certain point he called me over and told me to look through the camera viewfinder and see what he had done. But the lens was closed. "Wait till I open it for you . . ."

Out of the darkness the image of the Powell-Jesus emerged and struck me immobile. Those eyes. The same eyes that look upon us from our infancy, whether to comfort us or to make us know that they stand close by at every moment of our lives, whatever we do and wherever we hide.

The seamstress noticed a thread that was still attached to the veil and ran into the shot and started biting vigorously. Then she saw Powell's face and eyes under the lights and with that makeup. She stopped, petrified, and turned, "But he is Jesus!" And for several seconds she didn't know whether to go ahead with her work or fall on her knees.

And so, that day we all knew that the actor for our Jesus had been found or, more exactly, "had been sent to us."

The burden put on this man was not enviable. His responsibility toward us, toward the public, and to himself was immense. Powell was not only called upon to offer his face and voice to interpret the role but to live long months, perhaps years, in a working adventure that could be the heaviest and most fatiguing of his life. He was called on to give us an image of God convincing at the same time to hundreds of millions of people who had already forged one in their hearts, jealously guarded and defended in different degrees by all. He would have to give telling voice to the "divine words" while facing abnormal pain and sacrifice not normally asked of an actor.

And from the first phases of our work we were blessed with an extraordinary union of inspiration and of will that stayed with us through the long labor. We all still feel it today and I believe will do so all our lives. With Powell we found an abiding friendship that rejoices all of us every time we meet, even now, so long after the job has been done.

Robert Powell is a man utterly dedicated to his profession and rigorously disciplined. He is typical of English actors, who, once convinced of the rightness and necessity of the task, give themselves without reserve. During the entire shooting there was not a single problem, a word, a solution reached together, to which he did not dedicate himself with total absorption.

Take, for example, the scenes on the Way to the Cross and the Crucifixion. We were shooting them from the middle of January to the first days of February at Sousse in northern Tunisia. And that country at that time of the year certainly does not have a tropical climate. The local people were saying that this January of '76 was the coldest in their memory. We were swept by freezing winds and rains, with skies always carrying black clouds (skies that the Crucifixion called for). It was at this time that we decided to shoot the scene.

Powell had to drag the beam to which he would be nailed through the streets of Sousse (a real wooden beam, not the plastic one he had been offered, as it is a scene that had to come through as true, with all the actual torture it would call for) and mount the cross nude.

He agreed to being bound with rough ropes, just as was done

with the condemned in those days, with nails in his hands, simulated, of course, but which rendered him helplessly immobile—the most tormenting pain of one crucified.

The whole scene was shot so close to real life that Powell's example made everyone's emotions burst, even the most skeptical and knowledgeable. The crowd of extras and actors were gripped by a kind of collective despair. The Tunisians, who didn't realize it was a play, saw only the reality of the punishment—a bloodied man nailed to a cross. They believed it was all really happening.

From the moment we chose Robert Powell for the part we began to work with him and to prepare him in countless ways. When his theater engagement in London was through, Powell married, and I sent him and his wife to my house in Positano. There he could relax, regain his strength, and lose that "white worm" complexion, as it is called by English actors who spend their lives in the darkness of London theaters.

There was another reason for my concern. Powell's eyes were for me the principal medium of communication between him and the public—crystal eyes that pierce you, sending fire through your eyes to the very brain. The effect can be most disturbing and accounts for the charisma that this man exercises on all those who meet him. Already, his eyes, so sensitive in the screen test with Nannuzzi's gentle lighting, had shown signs of discomfort. I began to feel a growing preoccupation with what would happen when he had to face the African sun. At Positano he could begin to accustom himself to this kind of light.

Meanwhile the unit was now in Morocco, and at the end of September we had begun to shoot. It was at about this time that Powell joined us. We were filming the Nazareth scenes, the entire story of Mary and Joseph preceding the birth. This meant that he would not have to be called to work for a good month at least.

He was with us constantly watching the work in progress and studying my approach with the actors. He soon made friends with cast and crew, and they grew to know and love him.

When it came to his first scene, Jesus being thrown out of the synagogue, he was ready. He had become, with no need of recourse to artifices, that image we had all sensed on the day of the screen test so long ago.

The ability of the actors (a disposition that in truth we all have

Jesus by Franco Zeffirelli

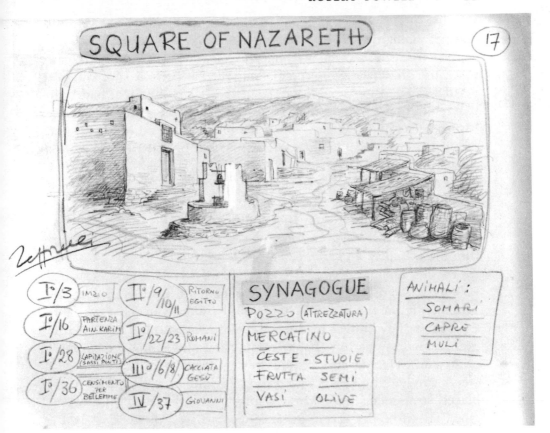

SQUARE OF NAZARETH 17

Zeffirelli

I°/3 INIZIO	II°/9/10/11 RITORNO EGITTO	SYNAGOGUE	ANIMALI:
I°/16 PARTENZA AIN-KARIM	II°/22/23 ROMANI	POZZO (ATTREZZATURA)	SOMARI
I°/28 LAPIDAZIONE (SASSI PINTI)	III°/6/8 CACCIATA GESÙ	MERCATINO	CAPRE
I°/36 CENSIMENTO PER BETLEMME	IV/37 GIOVANNI	CESTE - STUOIE	MULI
		FRUTTA SEMI	
		VASI OLIVE	

more or less) to bring about a complete change in themselves is well known. Often it is incredible and miraculous, permitting them to become, in effect, another person, another personality as real as their own. Pirandello, as a writer (to name one of many), made it a key theme in his plays, and it became an obsession with him. And I have had frequent experiences of it. The most sensational instance I recall is that of Maria Callas, who, at the beginning of her spectacular career, was terribly obese. She made up her mind to change. At that time Audrey Hepburn was in Rome to make *Roman Holiday*. Miss Callas conceived a desperate envy of the actress's grace and elegance, and she was determined to become like her. She kept her photograph in her dressing room, on the piano, in her boudoir, her bathroom; she underwent massages and cruel diets, and when we saw her again after less than a year she had effectively become another woman.

Not that she became a Hepburn exactly, but she had the gestures, the dress; she wore the makeup of that actress: she had, in a word, become that type of woman. It was as if that goal had been planted in the mind and the body's cells obeyed the mind's design. Just so with Powell. Little by little, having studied images of Christ, of ancient Hebrews, of the apostles, I found him at the end of this long wait ready to begin work.

Sometimes Powell would have reservations, but for the most part they concerned the text, the words to be chosen, the English translation of Jesus' words. There were translations that were awkward for oral delivery, too cold and solemn, words that didn't capture the actuality and immediacy of the original.

For the English text of the Gospels we were using a beautiful volume of translations from various periods, printed in parallel columns. From time to time we would choose the most recitable translation. Powell was reading (the Gospels), and I often saw him preoccupied by matters that were puzzling him, things he couldn't quite grasp. He was sure he couldn't get them across to the public convincingly. The Gospel according to John is obscure in many places, so immersed was the disciple in his transcendent and abstract vision of the mysteries and events he narrated. Certain set repetitions, the mysterious profundity of the writing, would make it difficult for anyone delivering the lines. "If I don't thoroughly understand what I have to speak, if I don't grasp it so as to live it within me, how can the public understand it sitting out there in the theater or turning on the television? If I have understood it well, only then I can make others understand it, too," said Powell.

Those were precisely the problems that we had discussed at length. I was obliged to put on film the message and the divine words of Jesus. To avoid the most difficult obstacles, to withdraw myself from this responsibility, was too unthinkable. I explained to Powell that Jesus often alternated his thoughts, in words most comprehensible to the minds of those who heard him, with matters of the highest theological significance, and often the apostles didn't understand. So true is this that disputes constantly arose even among them; just as is happening with us, because we, too, as they, are incapable of comprehending it entirely. But Jesus reassured them, saying that one day, when their minds had been opened by the power of the Holy Spirit, they would then understand . . .

Powell began to laugh: "But will he send the Holy Spirit to us? How can we find Jesus to understand him, if not even the apostles who were with him succeeded in that?"

Quip for quip. I could only repeat for him the words of Pascal: "Dear Robert, if you are searching for Jesus that means you have already found him."

After this great performance, Robert Powell will surely go on to many other parts, many other characterizations in films and the theater—very different, of course—because of the desire this actor has not to remain a prisoner of the "awesomeness" of Jesus, perhaps to roles completely opposite. But this experience will have stamped the life of the actor and the man with a mark of nobility that will stand against time and events.

Excerpt from a Letter to Suso Cecchi d'Amico, July 6, 1976:

Most serious is that with only a few days from starting to film, I have not yet found all locations, all the exteriors. We have decided with Labella to shoot the first part of the film in Morocco, beginning with Nazareth, the opening of the story.

Religious and government authorities have at last granted us, with remarkable understanding and generosity, the necessary authorizations. We will continue to stay in Morocco until the vigil of the Nativity and then move on to Tunisia, where I count on finding all the other locations I need to construct, on the best sites—the Temple of Jerusalem, the Tower of Antonius, the wall of Jerusalem, the interiors of Herod the Great's palace and Herod Antipas's palace, the synagogue at Nazareth, the rooms and great hall of Pilate, the room of the Last Supper, the house of Matthew, and those of Peter, Elizabeth, Joseph. . . .

We leave for Tunisia tomorrow, myself, Labella, Nannuzzi, our head of production, Luciano Piperno, and the other production assistants. These will be the final days of a preparation that has gone on for over a year: a handful of crucial days. In a little more than two months the cameras will begin to roll, and *Jesus* will emerge from the limbo of many projects to become, little by little, a film. The most exciting and the most awesome, looking up from the foot of the mountain to the top, that I have ever faced up to now. The summit seems far off, now, like a mirage.

Excerpt from a Letter to Lila DeNobili, July 1975:

I am approaching the date set for beginning the filming. Delays due to certain "political" confusion, to waverings, to second thoughts of him who wove the financial web of this enterprise, have bogged down our preparations.

Marcel and Sabbatini [my two costume designers for the film] are trying desperately to have ready on time the thousands of costumes that have to be cut, sewn, and aged so they won't look as though they have just been taken off the hangers in wardrobe but worn daily by real people in everyday life. The handwoven fabrics, ordered in Morocco and Tunisia, were delivered two months overdue. For costuming our crowds there is no other solution than to drag a tailor shop along with us from location to location, as we will do with the carpentry department, so that we will be assured of on-the-spot expertise in emergencies, and that will produce in record time the weekly and monthly changes and restorations that might be necessary. A pity you can't be with us.

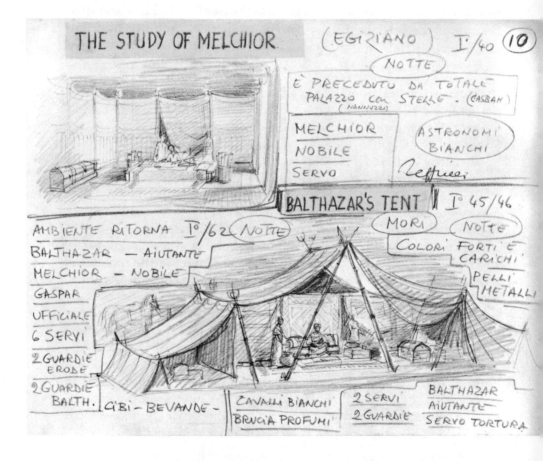

CHAPTER 10

The Messianic Expectation

The tribes of Israel were moved by a visceral mysticism; the Scriptures were their humus, the element in which they lived and to which they turned with all their hearts. The feeling of being a chosen people, of having for their own a holy and extraordinarily rich Law, which no other people had ever had, was a patrimony that belonged to every Jew, the poor and the powerful alike, and made everyone an heir to this enormous treasure. It made them stronger than any adversity. That which is today still their lasting heritage was the same massive moral block of granite before which Jesus found himself.

Just about every Jew who could read, thanks to his daily exposure to the Scriptures, knew that the answer to every spiritual question and every problem of life was contained in the Old Testament. And they could all recite it from memory, as of course was the case with the sacred texts and great epic poems of the ancient world down to the Renaissance, times in which knowledge had to be retained in the mind. "The cultivation of memory" was a gift that now, with our easy access to the printed word, to radio, television, and tape recorders, we are destroying. We don't even remember our own telephone numbers.

Constant debate and discussion on the possible interpretation of prophetic texts, swift comparison of one book, one text, with another—their dialectic was exceptionally refined, and at least half the day was dedicated to this virtuoso's exercise of interpretation, dialectic, and memory.

At the particular moment in history in which Jesus was born, along with religious controversies there were debates on the attitude to be taken toward the Romans, hated because they were conquerors and because they were pagans. It was a time, then, in which minds were agitated by the hope, the certainty, even, of resolving the many complicated political problems. And to resolve them, they turned to their faith in the prophets, they relied on the promises, the signs, the heritage of the Scriptures.

They were an aroused people, intractable, insuppressible. Taking literally the word of Scripture "if the Gentile invades your home, you have the right to kill him," they feared neither torture nor massacre and didn't hesitate to oppose the foreigners.

But apart from this, there was an educational aspect that set the Jews apart. Immersed in a world of words, the Torah, they had nothing else to attach themselves to, no images, no enticements of beauty, no allowments of luxury. The Torah, the Torah alone, was the subject of their conversation, and it was carefully read from beginning to end only to be reread once more.

With everybody living in messianic expectations, in fond anticipation of a guide able to give a new direction to the course of their history, they anxiously awaited a new David, another Solomon. But since David was born a shepherd, the notion that the Messiah could be born anywhere was a common persuasion, and so the expectation was alive and vibrant in every household. Every boy-child might be the Messiah, every girl-child might be the mother of the Messiah, every son, potentially, the carrier of this longed-for prodigy. One must insist upon this concept, this hope of the Hebrew people, because the character of Mary cannot be understood except in this context.

Mary was one of the countless girls nurtured in this hope. Joachim and Anne were very devout. They were steeped in the spirit of the Scriptures and dedicated to the precepts of the holy books. A fundamental rule concerned the division of the day into three parts—eight hours of sleep or rest, eight of labor or activities, eight of prayer, that is, discussion upon Scriptures to keep alive in every child of Israel the Mosaic message. And so, from her earliest years, Mary would inevitably have been present at those discussions and those prayers and, even while playing in a corner of the room, would have overheard all these things. The concepts, the ideas, the expectations, had to have been entering into her mind, sometimes without her being aware of it. And probably from the time she was a little one she harbored the hope, as did all her companions, of being the chosen one. But she! Why she? Out of all the people of the world, all the women of the world, must the divine design single out this modest little family group on the outskirts of Galilee?

The divine ray alighted upon this family, this city, this child out of an incomprehensible, mysterious design. And I like to think of Mary as a lovely, very special, very sensitive little girl from her earliest years.

Who knows what ran through her mind. Surely hers was perceptive, alert to the word of Scripture and more impressionable than others. But what does that mean? Simply a tenacious dream, a clinging to God's inner call? Spiritually sensitized and predisposed, we summon the spirit into us, we call upon it to the point of accentuating its power.

Parapsychology tells us of beings particularly receptive to spiritual vibrations, having a highly developed capacity for resonating to the mind and soul of other beings. Mary was not an ecstatic, but surely she must have been attuned and receptive to a transcendental message.

The announcement made to Mary opens up a very difficult area in the Gospel narrative. The dogma of Mary's virginity has spawned endless discussion, denial, and affirmation. It is interesting to read in the Koran one of the most peremptory rejections of that skepticism and incredulity that opposes the mystery of virginal conception on the dubious grounds of human logic.

The Koran says: "You ask how could life be born of the womb of a virgin. . . . To God anything is possible." In the film, I have chosen to respect the great mystery and to depict it through Mary's act of faith, and that of Anne, her mother, and of Joseph, who accepted this mystery uneasily at first, and then with complete conviction of mind and heart.

This way, our doubts are left outside the door of the little cottage of Nazareth where Mary, and she alone, receives the message that both frightens and thrills her.

We spectators do not hear the voice of the angel, the messenger sent by God, but only Mary's answers, at first timid and uncertain, at the end firm and secure.

In the film, as in the Gospel, Mary appears only at certain moments, but crucial moments, such as the Annunciation, the Crucifixion, and the Descent from the Cross. I depicted the wedding of Joseph and Mary with utter realism, which I was able to capture thanks to the participation of the people of Fertassa and the model of their primitive nuptial ceremonies, even today in every respect just like the ancient Jewish rites.

The figure of the mother, as I said, occupies little space in the Gospel.

The Gospel, for me, is really a diary of the years of Jesus' preaching, the history of his adulthood. There are several instances that indicate that Jesus' rapport with his family was simply nil. They wanted him to come home, to come back and help his family, especially since he had achieved success and had many disciples, who most likely gave him contributions (it seems that Judas was his treasurer). And just as the mother of the Zebedees was concerned about the economical and social future of her sons, it is quite possible even the aging Mary went to find Jesus to ask him to think of her and of his own. But she was obliged to wait day in and day out while the apostles made up their minds to advise the Master of her presence. They asked him to see and to listen to his mother, so patiently waiting for him. Instead, Christ looked upon them severely and spoke: "Who is my mother? Who are my brothers? Whoever does the will of my Father in Heaven, he is my brother and sister and mother." And he apparently sends Mary away empty-handed.

Against this shift from light to shadow, from belief to doubt, I set the lonely and intimate drama of Joseph—many consider him an Essene, a Pharisee of love. Actually, Joseph had to be a very pious man—to accept, after some reluctance, the story that Mary tells about her maternity, and then to participate eagerly at the birth of a child not his own. Nevertheless, it is understandable that at first he would have been shocked when told of the pregnancy of his young spouse and have been on the verge of sending her away. Anne's patience, her warmth, was needed to assure him he should keep the girl, but when, finally, through divine inspiration, he realized he was involved with a child of heaven, a son beyond all normal human destiny, he was moved and delighted and gave thanks to the Lord. Even he had to know that something supernatural was happening when he saw the shepherds rush to the cave. They were troubled and excited by a vision, by a mysterious voice that directed them to that humble dwelling to admire and to adore the Son of God. And then, with the visit of the Magi, every lingering doubt vanished. Their words of advice to take his wife and child and flee to Egypt because Herod's rage would soon be aroused he obeyed at once, fearfully, yes, but thrilled over what he now has as a clear command from the Lord.

A difficult figure, Joseph—complicated and at times uncertain. I removed him from the scene just before Jesus approached the Jordan.

Nevertheless, I have taken special care to present his story and so hold to the goal I had set out for myself, that is, to show that the Gospel is not a collection of fairy tales à la Andersen or La Fontaine but a series of plausible events—even though presented in a schematic or hagiographic way and, often even crudely. It is somewhat like the famous seven days of Creation in Genesis. Clamorously rejected by unbelievers, they have been verified scientifically—the order indicated in the account being accurate but the time periods contracted, as is often the way in the Scriptures.

But the story of Joseph and Mary enabled me to present the true nature of the Jewish people and, at the same time, to throw light on our sad alienation from a world of purity and of values that inspired the thought and actions of Jesus' contemporaries.

From some hints in texts later than the Gospels, one can deduce that Joseph was a man of extraordinary mysticism who had gone beyond the already lofty spiritual plane of the people of Nazareth and had dedicated his whole life to exalting the word of God.

Joseph, a member of the tribe of David, was a carpenter, which at that time in Galilee meant a practitioner of a noble craft, and for that he was highly respected. And it was he who had to show this world the first act of faith when he said to Mary, "I believe you, I believe in this mystery," and from that act of faith countless others emerged, germinated by the flame of Christian love.

I repeat that I wanted to present Joseph, not as a ridiculed husband, but as a man completely permeated by the sense of a mystery too towering for his mind but not for his heart, a man who saw his faith rewarded here on earth, immediately, in the prodigious story of that infant born as his son.

The birth of Jesus, the place of his birth, Bethlehem, that census of Augustus, politically motivated but divinely ordained, are coincidences that some reject but that history, on the one hand, and tradition, on the other, support.

The sacred texts have always indicated a tiny Judean town, Bethlehem-Ephrata, as the birthplace of the Messiah, he who would set Israel free. The decree ordering the tribe-by-tribe census arrived at Nazareth. Joseph was not from Nazareth but belonged to the tribe of David and his forefathers—the whole tribe were away there in that area of Judea—therefore the young couple were obliged to set out for the place of their origin.

The kind of census, the census itself, the journey to Bethlehem, many scholars challenge. They call it absurd, almost brutal, a census that forces people to travel hundreds of miles to inscribe their names on a register, creating intolerable confusion in the towns and along the road. The reasonable thing would be to conduct the census at the place where each one lived.

The experts have gone so far as to deny that Nazareth even existed at the time, that it dates to at least a century later, since there is no mention of that name in the literature of the first century of our era, neither Hebrew, Roman, nor Greek.

For years they have been battling in vain over this story like all punctilious experts who know everything except what really matters. But I feel that this marvelously poetic touch brings into the narrative a dimension so lofty that it can't have been randomly invented by petty politicians and clever manipulators of history. Furthermore, why could it not have been true? Unfortunately, those whose minds are shut to reasons of the spirit are always looking for petty material motives, shabby reasoning, in terms of human speculation, to explain human history, while every page of the Gospel is permeated with poetry and a most fervid faith. It is just this vision of the world's history that in the end is more true.

Gospel criticism finds in the Evangelists a compulsion to compose a narrative dominated by prophecies that *had* to be verified, and this alarms the suspicious. For them certain episodes appear to be more legends: the Magi's visit, the appearance of the miraculous Star, or the slaughter of the innocents. And so, there can be no connection between these tales and the true history of Jesus. In fact, the most ancient tradition—that found in Mark—ignores the journey to Bethlehem, and even John doesn't mention it.

But in the end, we must be persuaded that it all could be true, and I would say far more true than mere fantasy. The plain fact is that the primitive tradition that gave birth to the Gospels was not interested in the "hidden life" of Jesus—that long stretch of his life from his birth to his baptism by John.

"The Christological development which is found in Paul and the

Johannine literature quickly deterred the faithful from any inquiry about the human infancy of the 'Savior' who was always thought of from an eschatological perspective," Guignebert observes.

In any case, the appearances of a star or comet in those years has recently been confirmed by scholars.

This particular episode being exact, why couldn't all the others recorded by the evangelists also be correct? If the year of the birth of Jesus is disputable, that is because even the apostles, like all the ancient world, had a very vague idea of years and of time. Dates were imprecise, even for the Greeks and the Romans. Dates such as the olympiad and the founding of the empire were not recorded exactly. For that matter, even today in many parts of the world you find people who don't even know how old they are.

Since the computation was done many years after the life of Christ, it was probably in error. Actually, it seems that Jesus was born six years before the accepted date, because Herod the Great died in 6 "B.C." Therefore, Jesus would really have been about 39, not 33, at his death.

Joseph experienced another confirmation of his faith during the Circumcision, which many think took place at the Temple of Jerusalem, only about eleven kilometers from Bethlehem. The mysterious fact is that at the moment that this infant, touched by the blade of circumcision, let out a cry, the sound reached the ears of an old man, a wise old man who had devoted his life to the Scriptures and was reciting them, just like some men who, until recently, roamed around inside our churches or loitered in the church squares. This old man hears the infant's cry, and suddenly he rises and, as though struck by lightning, runs into the synagogue shouting: "I thank you, O God, for having permitted me at the end of my life to see the king who will save the world from its sins." He takes the newborn into his arms and gazes on him with love and devotion; he returns him to the arms of the mother, and fixing his eyes on Mary, he murmurs, "A sword will pierce your heart," foreseeing in an instant the sorrow that will fall upon the mother in fulfillment of the tragic human destiny of Jesus.

In my research, I did not attempt to press all these incidents into a realistic form. I preferred to present them as an evocative story, because this is actually an area of the Gospel that calls for our poetic cooperation, our imagination, to make it alive.

A pity one can't see it all with innocent eyes, like those of infants.

I envisioned not three but ten, a hundred, Magi coming from Asia Minor and Africa, attracted by the comet. I saw a kind of convention of these sages at the juncture where the star brought their paths together. Each one with his own calculations, each with his own prophecy, but all agreed on one point. The appearance of the star had to coincide with a most important event.

I saw them intent upon reassuring themselves, as befits good astronomers, that nothing happens by chance, least of all a celestial phenomenon. The stars are not the cold, icy, invincible creatures they may appear to be, but rather creatures made of matter that pulse and radiate mysterious energies, so much so that what occurs in the skies is always a message for all mankind.

I believe in seeing Herod, weary of kinsmen, servants, and counselors constantly repeating, "People talk of nothing else, only this star," turning to his advisors, his scientists, his sages, who all confirm the popular belief in the star, until finally Herod shouts, "I will pull down this star, I will rip it from heaven, I will crush it under my heel. . . . And meanwhile I will eliminate all the infants born this year."

But the Magi, who had heard whispers of this, had time to alert Joseph; and so his family is already on the road when, behind them, the bloody tragedy of Bethlehem is unleashed. All the male infants up to two years old are slaughtered by Herod's soldiers, in homes, in the squares, the streets, the fields.

The most tragic aspect is that Jesus, in coming to earth, had to provoke this hecatomb of sacrifices, a destiny of blood. The slaughter of the innocents reveals in such a holocaust one of the reasons why the Son of God became incarnate. And he, in his turn, would repay his own blood as a sacrifice for others. And all this blood, which opens and closes the story of Christ, flows out as a rich, sacrificial stream over the Christian faith.

If one then reflects on the holocaust of the martyrs after Christ, witnessing to their faith, one realizes how this bloody story might begin with the birth of Christ.

From infancy, Jesus would have been introduced to a most profound and sensitive understanding of the Scriptures. We know, in fact, of one incident, transmitted somewhat in legend form—Jesus at only twelve years of age conversing with the learned rabbis. At twelve, Jesus was accepted into the "adult" community of the synagogue, which meant he had the right to discuss the Scriptures. That he knew them better than many others is quite possible, his having been intensely trained during those twelve years by that exceptional master Joseph. The fact, then, that he might have discussed scriptural questions in the Temple is more than plausible. Besides, humanity has shown us other youthful prodigies, such as the young Mozart, an extraordinary musician at the age of five.

But from that moment, there is no mention of him. We know little of Nazareth even; we know nothing until the proclamation of his mission in the synagogue at Nazareth—the moment of his first step, his first grand, but scandalous, pronouncement.

Then the mission of Christ really begins, when he says, "From this moment the Kingdom of God is in your midst."

Jesus' presence in Nazareth presupposes that he had not abandoned his own country for mystical or religious experiences elsewhere, pilgrimages, months of fasting or the desert's solitude, or concourse with others gifted with the spirit of prophecy or miracles.

This is one of the discoveries that came to me as I was shooting the film and gave the simplest possible reply to all the age-old speculations about the "hidden years" of Jesus.

Jesus presumably stayed with his father, helping him in his work, joining him in his religious practices and discussing them with him. This had to be the history of Joseph. I chose a Greek actor, Yorgo Voyagis, to play Joseph—a young man not at all like the traditional image of a meek, emasculated Joseph.

I immediately hung two curls in front of the lobes of his ears, indicating a certain type of orthodoxy. Actually, many Jews wear them to indicate visibly their complete dedication to religious life and to the Scriptures. During prayer the finger kept searching for these circles to curl them; the more the hair was thus curled, the more numerous the circlets of a curl, the stronger the devotion of him who wore them. They were, then, a distinction, a way of relating to prayer, just like the "beads" strung on little chains that the Arabs slip through their fingers—the origin, incidentally, of our rosary.

Further Notes of a Journey:

Seen from the top of the hill where the sovereigns of the Merimide dynasty are buried, Fez, the cultural center of Morocco, can resemble ancient Jerusalem if one is careful to find the right settings.

In ancient Medina we visit the dyers' part of the town: an indescribable spectacle, an explosion of splendid colors and atrocious odors. In a little shop we discover various objects belonging to an abandoned synagogue: seven-branched candelabra and an authentic collection of very ancient rolls of the Torah on parchment. Our producer was ecstatic after getting involved in a fierce verbal duel with the shrewd merchant; in the end his supply of *dirham* was substantially depleted, but he was the happy owner of the scrolls. They will be precious for us in creating atmosphere and authenticity in the synagogue scenes. Small steps these, but important along the path to that truth that I must reach at all costs.

In the dense center of Medina of Meknes, I found the house of Jairus, the father of the girl Jesus called back to life with the Aramaic words *"Talitha cumi"* (little girl, arise), which the Gospel has handed down to us.

Ancient Turkish baths can be transformed into the offices of the scribe

THE SERMON ON THE MOUNT

OF SUN
LOUDS —

...deal; there is a cupola ...of a star. We will have ...down the wood oven ...stop. We will have to ...ousands of beard clip- ...g shaved both before

...ves me an idea for the ...' I am thinking of the ...oncentric circles on the ...nd to each individual: ...nd that space and that ...even unto us.

The Shrine of Moulay Idriss provides us an ideal ambience for the grand choral sequence of the multiplication of loaves and fishes. A kind of band of miracle seekers is always wandering around that area; most probably it is the equivalent of the crowd of deprived and hapless people who followed the Nazarene, dragging behind them their hopes and their sorrows, expecting to be made free at the touch of those hands, hands capable of unparalleled actions.

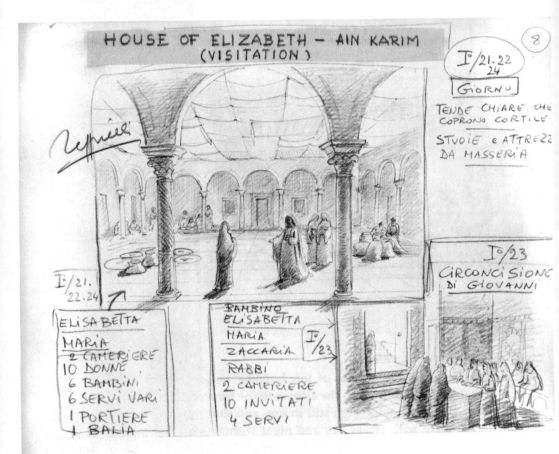

CHAPTER 11

Mary

The Madonna was a casting problem that, at first, as with the part of Jesus, I found almost insoluble.

I had looked everywhere for the right actress—Sardinia, Greece, Spain, in every corner of this world. Since the character of Mary does not speak much, language was no problem. Mary speaks some words at the beginning but then is silent: once her function—giving birth to God—has been completed, she doesn't open her mouth again. She observes, she listens passively, sorrowfully; she remains merely a presence, a presence that finally bursts into tears. All this lessened my responsibility for a speaking actress, but on the other hand, I had to have a convincing *presence.*

Mary could not be a flighty girl. So often, when we look at the magnificent abstraction of our great painters and sculptors, we tend to see her as crystallized in time and matter. But it is one thing to have a block of marbles in which the contours of youth remain unchanged, a mirror of untouched purity that this very marble renders deathless and transcendent, as in Michelangelo's *Pietà.* It is another thing to have a woman, a live girl, who, when photographed and projected on television, can retain that magic—the magic of a fresh countenance and uncontaminated heart.

The woman Mary, was actually, and in the dramatic action had to be, a baffling character, enigmatic, a person you don't know how to categorize once and for all.

When you have that face in front of you in the silence of the chapel in St. Peter's, a ray of light falling upon it from above, you remove it entirely from any human context, from all reality. But when you see it in the world of Nazareth, with the chickens, the little donkey, at the loom, during the engagement ceremony, or on the journey to Bethlehem, you need human qualities approaching the sublime as convincing as possible, and beauty, too, not artificial or disturbing, but a true inner beauty. Furthermore, she must be convincing as a young woman and as a mature woman, but, most of all, as a mother. It is always terribly difficult for a serious actress to settle for cinemagraphic deceits. So it was imperative then that her aging should develop within, from her spirit, and that it should show in her appearance with a minimum of makeup.

Here again, the eyes are particularly important—that inner light, the enigma, the mystery in their depths.

Extensive research in the Mediterranean area, in Israel, in Spain, in North Africa, and finally in the Atlas Mountains, where I found marvelous young girls but they were all so *native,* they could give nothing in front of the camera. I finally went back to my original idea: an *actress,* a particular one with those special characteristics.

So, at first, I thought of having an unknown actress play the youthful Mary and give the part of the older Mary to Irene Papas. I launched a campaign in Greece to find a girl who would have all the features of Irene Papas at fifteen years.

Hundreds applied, but none was satisfactory. Then I remembered Olivia Hussey, an actress very dear to me, who had played Juliet in my *Romeo and Juliet.*

Seven years had passed, but she still radiated the bloom of youth. Still the same soft camellia skin, the innocent face, the same dreamy wonderment. But within, Olivia had seen and had lived through both happiness and sorrow. She had married, had been greatly disillusioned. She had a three-year-old child and had been divorced, but despite it all, she remained fresh and unspoiled in spirit.

Her youthful freshness, combined with a sense of maturity, offered a very interesting solution. After doing a screen test of her, both as a girl and as a mature woman, I knew I could not have found anyone better. In fact, with a wisdom that I could call more than professional, welling up directly from spiritual depths, she gave me everything I had been looking for in a young Madonna—"the most ancient in the world." Mary had to appear as a mixture—I won't say ambiguous, but ambivalent—of the mystery and the divine light that falls upon her unspoiled life.

The mystery is difficult, almost impossible, to portray except through almost imperceptible changes in the face, in a glance, in a smile, the mystery that the camera can capture in the features, the lights and shadows of the face, while the divine comes only from a profound inner persuasion that the eyes must convey.

The young Mary is just right, she is an image of sweetness and strength together. Olivia has even become a Jew. She had enormous problems to solve, moments practically impossible to interpret, for example, the impulse of joy when, because of Elizabeth's pregnancy, she is certain that the announcement of her own forthcoming maternity—communicated by means of a mysterious voice—is not a deception.

"I have been chosen, I!" She is completely Jewish, steeped in this expectation, and cries with joy at that revelation. "It is I, it is I. I am the chosen of the chosen," she exclaims. And with that, Olivia captures the happiness of the moment in a delightful, exultant leap of joy.

Olivia is a girl who, curiously enough, has for many years been engrossed, not with parapsychology, but with the fascination of Eastern mysticism, which has overrun the Anglo-Saxon world—with the gurus, some phonies, others not, who somehow succeed in spreading contentment and happiness. I have known many broken people who have found a reasonable solution to their problems with the help of a guru, and in the confused jungle in which we live, this spiritual source, though passive, permits them to engage in the life of the spirit.

I have always teased Olivia about it, but this intimate contact with Hindu spirituality, acknowledged also by Paul VI on the occasion of his visit to India, served us well in our efforts to portray the character of Mary. Because, when she had to face the mystery, or other difficult moments of her role—and they are all difficult—she withdrew into a kind of Yoga ecstasy, eventually to burst forth with a power due not simply to the artistry of a skilled actress but to the eruption of her entire being releasing itself. Her whole spirit burst forth and was captured on film.

I had the good luck to find the same intensity in the Descent from the Cross scenes, where she created something truly rare in the cinema. She was so totally immersed in her role, in her world of utter grief, that at the climax, sobbing in the rain pelting the lifeless body of her martyred son, she drew him to herself with amazing strength. Olivia actually lifted up Robert Powell, a seventy-kilo man, as though she were really taking an infant into her motherly embrace. A moving scene, perhaps the most dramatic of them all.

Olivia was the center of some curious episodes in Morocco and Tunisia. There were Muslims, men of vivid faith, who absolutely refused to look at her, because to them the person of Mary was almost more sacred than Jesus himself.

Those few who dared to lift their heads to look at her did so with immense reverence, but most of the time they turned away from her immediately.

From a Letter of February 7, 1975, to My Sister Fanny:

Pippo discovered a girl about fifteen years, a veritable fawn, timid and curious at once; an amazing face, set with intense, black, liquid, and darting eyes. An image of the young Mary. The interview was quickly over; when he had finished the job of photographing her, her brother intervened to say no to any notion, now or ever, of having his sister take part in a film.

But walking with these two youths we passed an entrance to a house in which the sounds of music and dancing could be heard. By special favor, we were allowed in to take part in what was the prologue to a nuptial ceremony. A very young bride was dressed in a wedding gown, adorned, and covered with jewels lent to her by all the women of the village to make her appear even more beautiful and rich. Just then her mother was putting a veil over her and signaling a group of young people, also with faces veiled, who were entering the courtyard carrying a kind of large tray. On this they sat the bride and then lifted her, supporting the tray with raised arms. Only upon arriving at the house of the groom could they lower the bride to the ground, and all could unveil.

I took photographs and made sketches. I want to re-create in detail this pure joy and innocence of this nuptial rite. The entire countryside fills the houses of the newlyweds and participates in their simple feast.

Mary and Joseph would be at home here, in the midst of this people who still drink from goatskin wine containers and retire when the sun goes down, measuring their days by the rhythm of the muezzin's call to remember God and Mohammed, his Prophet.

CHAPTER 12

The Jordan

It has been said that the first Christians manipulated the life of Jesus to make it coincide with old Testament prophecies, further, that the concern of the disciples and of Saint Paul, and of all who were equipped to recount the earthly deeds of Jesus was just that, stubbornly and relentlessly comparing the salient moments of Christ's life with what Elias, Isaiah, and the other prophets had foretold. This incessant and meticulous task was necessary because among the Jews a man could acquire credibility and become the Messiah on condition that his deeds and words coincide with the words and the writings of the prophets.

Opponents of the Gospel contend that the task of linking Jesus to the prophecies was methodically done, though sometimes contradictory. In matching episodes from the Old Testament to the New there are surprising analogies at the moment of the Crucifixion, such as "they divided my garments beneath the gallows," "they cast dice," "a lance will pierce my side."

In my film, I purposely omitted these punctilious references to prophecies. The prophetic visions are echoed in the sequences of this film, but they are the great discourses: those that keep expectation alive, that refer to the Birth, to the triumphal Entry into Jerusalem, and, finally, to the Death and Resurrection.

For the Crucifixion, I preferred to create a grand dramatic scene with the people of Israel as protagonists, a scene of profound tension, rather than indulge in details of the various prophecies. In doing this my hope was that the viewer's attention could be concentrated not on incidentals but on the central meaning of the Crucifixion—on God, who, to reconcile himself with mankind, sent his only

Son so that they might better understand his word, God, in a word, who has to immolate his Son so that this new pact might come about.

Israel was in desperate need of this new peace treaty to better understand itself. The chosen people had, in fact, arrived at a point of unimaginable confusion, particularly for them, the depositaries of the Law. The chaos provoked in the Sanhedrin by the rivalries of various leaders, the political compromises that they had to accept with the Roman occupation, the internal divisions, the Zealots who wound up becoming violent under the stimulus of mysticism—it all led to such confusion that someone was needed who could pick up the thread of social and political discourse, which was by that time quite abandoned.

In this atmosphere, at last, Jesus arrives, in the most unexpected manner, son of a carpenter, from Nazareth, the simplest little village in Galilee, a town of shepherds.

This we can say: Jesus was truly born on the day of his baptism, the day of his encounter with John the Baptist on the banks of the Jordan. It is actually the first time we meet him as an adult, among the penitents going to confess their sins and be cleansed in the river.

John notices this exceptional presence immediately and, deeply moved, exclaims: "It is I who should come to you to be baptized, and yet it is you who come to me." And Jesus replies: "Let us allow the Scriptures to be fulfilled." And he is baptized.

At that moment a voice is heard, which I imagine as resounding in John's inmost conscience and becoming the inner voice of the Baptist, a response of the spirit moved by the voice of God to the point of repeating, as though in ecstasy, the words: "This is my beloved Son in whom I am well pleased." After this joyful exclamation, John calls two of his followers, Andrew and Philip, and orders them:"Behold the Lamb of God, sent by God to take away the sins of the world. Follow him and not me. He will increase, while I can only decrease."

Thus, on the banks of the Jordan, spoke the greatest of the prophets in a period abounding with prophets, fanatics, madmen, and sects such as the Essenes, aloof even from the tribes of Israel in obsessive rites of cleanliness and continual purification. There are those who say that Jesus himself might have been part of the sect that exhibited another way of being a Jew. Someone has suggested that possibly John had been an Essene. There, by the Jordan, this

crucible of mystical and religious tension was molded—a phenomenon that seems to be found along the great rivers, the Ganges, for
instance, the Nile and the Euphrates. There is the bathing and
cleansing, the need for external cleanliness, and at the same time,
by analogy, internal purification. And it was also the rite of public
confession: to wash oneself while confessing one's sins aloud.

Baptism was a most important sacral gesture, the more so if
administered by a man of superior moral fiber such as John, who
was respected, too, by the authorities because of his holiness. For
this reason he had experienced no interference up to that time. They
looked on him as a mystic revolutionary, therefore harmless. His
attack on Herod was not socially or politically motivated. It was
solely moral, motivated by indignation at the king and at saving him
from eternal punishment for having taken Herodias, his brother's
wife, for his own. It especially outraged John because Herod was the
king and his conduct inevitably set an example for all. "If I don't
admonish you, I, too, will be responsible for your sins!" That was
John's conviction, which tended to make more difficult the scheming of Herodias, until the barbaric twist of the bitter and tragic
Salome incident that has evoked the inspiration of artists, poets, and
musicians.

The scene at the Jordan was shot later on, in Tunisia, because the
actors had to be in the water for long periods, and Michael York,
who played the Baptist, was not free until April.

It was filmed after Easter, at Gabès, where a huge oasis of more
than three hundred thousand palm trees creates an unbelievable
landscape around a gushing natural spring. Upstream from the
oasis, the spring forms a lagoon with water that is daily distributed
to one of the seven sections of the oasis, so that in the course of a
week all the areas are irrigated.

With heavy pressure on the local authorities, we obtained permission to divert all that water into its former natural bed, a kind
of dry wadi, and from the wadi, with a dam constructed by our
incomparable engineers, "our" Jordan was born.

All the citizens of Gabès, after undergoing a week of dryness,
contributed to the success of this difficult scene. The instant these
rushing waters, pure and fresh, returned to their natural course was
one of great joy for all, as though the landscape had been re-created
and restored to them. The whole scene was filmed in a general state
of euphoria.

From a Letter Written to My Sister Fanny, Easter 1976:

At Gabès, as in all the other regions of North Africa we visited in our work, we have come into contact with the purity and tenacity of popular religious sentiment, rare qualities in a world as skeptical and disenchanted as ours.

The life philosophy of this people, humble and mild, yet fierce in dedication to their traditions, has given us inspiration and encouragement.

Yesterday, Vincenzo Labella and I saw on the white wall of a hovel at the oasis of Gabès this strange inscription in Arabic and crude French: UN PAIN A PARTAGER OU ELLE S'ENVOLE. We then came upon the author, a bearded little man with wild but smiling eyes. We asked him what that "Elle" was, that "it" that would be snatched away if one refused to share one's bread with others. He stared at us for a moment. "Happiness," he replied.

CHAPTER 13

The Limitations of Film

Who then was this Jesus who presented himself to John on the banks of the Jordan? Was he *only* one of many penitents, a carpenter who had been working for thirty years and had then felt a need for purification, as so many in Israel? Or one who for some time had been initiated into some type of religious life and belonged to some strict sect? Or was he really a man already aware of his own destiny after having put himself to the test in the menacing solitude of the desert?

We cannot know. Moreover, all these suppositions flow together like several streams into one riverbed at that supreme moment in which he appears before John with the firm intention of revealing himself as Christ, guide, and Savior.

He was thirty (or thirty-six) years of age and quite mature for that period and culture. He was at the height of his intellectual and moral powers, and clearly, he looked to John to be the prophet who would launch his mission.

We cannot say how long Jesus traveled the country proclaiming the good news, but I think it may have been a fairly long period, despite those who prefer to limit his preaching to only a few months.

It could be, too, that many of the incidents located between the Jordan event and his death could have taken place earlier. For instance, the temptations in the desert Jesus would have been subjected to as a man, in all his human frailty, before being able to formulate and establish with precision his dual-natured identity, already intuited, but finally grasped through a special charism only after his confrontation with Satan.

As Dante descends through the hells down to the Devil and then returns to see the stars again, so Jesus confronts Satan in the desert, repulses him three times, and returns, strengthened for earthly parable. This episode of the Temptations, set by the Gospels against the background of prophecies, I filmed but, for a very definite reason, did not use in the final version.

Here, in fact, one arrives at pure mystery, and mystery is in itself beyond portrayal, especially in an art form so tenuous and limited as cinematography.

Much more effective were the many classical paintings of Satan, in which he was depicted with horns, because this suggestive image invited the viewer to throw open a window on mystery.

Cinema impedes the necessary concentration and, with that, the kind of participation indispensable for approaching the supernatural, the mysterious. Although I shot this sequence and it delighted many, I chose to cut it after long, anguished discussions with Labella, who was by my side every time we faced problems so decisive. The desert was impressive and the voice that resonated in that vast space became mysterious and disturbing; I had magnified the voice of Jesus. It was Jesus who uttered the words of the Devil as though he had captured them out of that space. An awesome, harsh, upsetting monologue ensued.

But Jesus' torment, too profound to be externalized, could confuse the viewer dangerously.

This was one of the instances in which the medium of film manifested its limitations. The effects were splendid, yes, but they seem contrived, ersatz, false.

This mystery I omitted, but there are others I hint at and leave to the faith and conscience of each to decide for or against. For example, I presented the Annunciation as a mystery. There's a young girl, awakened in the night, a breeze blowing through the window, she hears a voice that we do not hear, because it is addressed to her alone, a special rapport with the divine. The mother hears noise, hears the fuss, hears her daughter talking with someone, answering someone, and saying: "How can it be, I have never been touched by a man." The girl is on her knees and: "I am the handmaid of the Lord," she whispers, "I will do what the Lord wants."

This kind of mystery is more easily portrayed; I accept it, and display it with full responsibility. The viewer who goes along with this scene is led to believe that the girl heard things that we do not or for one who rejects the Gospel, that she is a fraud, that she has sinned and hasn't the courage to tell her mother.

Since Anne is not a mother of our times but a Jewish woman completely immersed in messianic expectations, she accepts this supernatural event immediately, with joy and pride. With us a question would occur at once: Who has the girl slept with? the gardener? the apprentice boy from the shop next door? Instead, Anne accepts her story with enthusiasm, especially because of another delightful detail recorded in the Gospel.

The little one does not actually say: "I am pregnant," but only: "I know that my cousin Elizabeth will bear a child." "But she is old," her mother replies, "she has never had children, and now it is too late." Mary answers immediately and notes the very day on which Elizabeth became pregnant.

Don't talk nonsense, her mother insists. But Mary persists in her version and is moved by a compulsion to go and find Elizabeth. At that moment word arrives that Elizabeth is indeed pregnant.

If the child is correct about Elizabeth's condition, her mother thinks, this other message is clearly true.

This type of mystery can be told by allowing the viewer total freedom to participate or not, to contribute to a ritual or to reject it. If the viewer and the actor do not work together, that mysterious space is not created, that curious rapport that is the very essence of theater. And of course we must remember that in the beginning all theatrical themes had a sacred and mystical character, inasmuch as they dealt with ancient tales or tribal rites dramatically re-enacted.

Today we employ a very sophisticated medium that, because it is mechanical, and because of its perfection (or imperfection in certain instances), doesn't help at all in communicating the incommunicable that, say, the Delphic oracle, uttering disjointed and muted words through a mask, was able to transmit to a predisposed and rapt viewer.

For this reason I quickly realized that the Temptation sequence could not be portrayed adequately, and I restricted myself to showing it by implication, it being common knowledge that such enlightened men went off into the desert to a hermitage, to be alone, to sensitize themselves, to communicate with God. They were completely alone, and woe if the slightest thing intruded—a noise, a flash, a gust of wind—to bring them back to earth! They ate locusts, drank water when it was available, renounced everything, because the desert's solitude was the way to make contact, the most intimate possible, with divinity.

Evidently Jesus, too, through his desert experiences and arduous tests of body and spirit, had sharpened and tempered his spiritual sensibilities and, when he felt ready, had presented himself at the synagogues in Nazareth and concluded his public reading with the remark: "Today the Scriptures have been fulfilled in your hearing." This was for the Jew a fearful blasphemy, because only on the day the Messiah had arrived would the Scriptures be automatically fulfilled.

The enraged bystanders throw him out of the synagogue. There is an uproar; a rabbi, who perhaps intuited something mysterious happening, tries to calm the crowd and says to Jesus: "No one has ever been a prophet in his own home."

Jesus then shakes the dust of Nazareth from his sandals and at that moment decides to go about preaching to the world.

CHAPTER 14

The Apostles

The dramatic episode at Nazareth signaled the beginning of Jesus' public career. He went immediately to Capernaum and began his preaching there with two problems to face: winning followers and selecting close disciples. Having made contact with the world, he took from it twelve men as so many symbols of humanity, each with a special and significant personality in the concert of the great human comedy.

What kind of men did Jesus want around him?

The very number twelve indicates a symbolic choice: the number of the tribes of Israel, the twelve signs of the zodiac.

Unfortunately, I was unable to tell each one's story; it would have taken nearly four hours of film to examine their origins, thought, spiritual characteristics, and special qualities, things that the Gospels touch upon only rarely and briefly. But I have made room for a couple of them: Peter, for instance, who links his destiny with Andrew's and John's; and Matthew, the tax collector, scourge of the fishermen of Capernaum, whom I envisioned as a personal enemy of Peter.

Then there were Andrew and Philip, whom Jesus met at the Jordan. But in my account I could only give them a brief scene: Jesus gazes at them, puts his hand on their shoulders, and says: "Follow me." We don't know where they were born; we know nothing of their character. We know only that Andrew also was a fisherman and he, too, had abandoned fishing to follow the Baptist, compelled by the intensity of his spiritual life.

Thus their story begins, each with his own personal concerns, his own particular character. Together they make up the ideal man.

I don't mean ideal for their virtues, but for the ensemble of their vices, defects, and qualities. They are the epitome of humanity.

It was intriguing to analyze which kind Jesus had chosen, what kind of man interested him. Bartholomew, for instance, was a physician but not particularly distinguished, more an herbalist, a pharmacist. Thaddeus was an artist, or rather an instrumentalist, a flutist and drummer. Then there was Matthew, an accountant, the practical man, a minor tyrant quite adept at collecting taxes in Nazareth. The limited scope and qualification of these men define, too, the very modest, limited horizons of that tiny world alongside a lake smaller than our Trasimeno.

Peter, though, was a rough man, with a large family to support. He was the chief of Capernaum's fishermen, depressed by the mood of those wretched times of crisis, poor catches, and heavy taxes—

lamenting it, cursing it, perhaps often striking his wife in rage and despair. And then drinking to forget it all.

Jesus had observed them; he had seen them in the crowd, and he took them for what they were—real men, earthy and sensitive, with a keen feel for reality. These were the men he needed. There was only one intellectual among them: John. His father, Zebedee, had planned for him a life of study. The good Zebedee was aware of John's intelligence and had spent a considerable sum to educate him, but John had seen salvation in Jesus and, with it, intellectual fulfillment and spiritual insight. He abandoned his studies, and from that moment was continually at Jesus' side, trying to plumb his every word—the most difficult, the most obscure.

Gripped, captured in this astonishing web of words, thoughts, deeds—not yet comprehending it all—they were delighted just to hear him. And while he often reproached them, jolted them, and chided them for their blindness about God's ways and for the ignorance that they repeatedly manifested, he always concluded by calming them, perhaps smilingly, and once again assuring them: "You will understand only at the end, but you *will* understand. Some day I will send the Holy Spirit upon you and then you will comprehend it all."

There are those curious, almost comical, incidents, too, of the mothers, the women who accompany the group, remaining cautiously at a distance, humbly apart, forming another, different little tribe but no less captivated by the Master's words. I see them following in the Lord's footsteps with household utensils, simple things—a soup bowl, a large spoon, a bag, a bundle on the end of a stick—women with a shawl that represented all their riches and served both to cover their heads and protect their shoulders from the winds off the Lebanon and as bedding for the night. During stopovers the women worked; they gathered grain, prepared bread, and knitted. They wore a seamless robe for Jesus like the one worn by the High Priest of Jerusalem, the tunic that will be torn by Caiaphas and will symbolize the definitive rejection of Jesus. They were a people without our needs; they slept and ate on the ground. A cave sufficed to make a house.

Little by little the popularity of Jesus grew, and so, too, did that cortege of miracle seekers who followed him. Perhaps also, through alms and offerings, a fund grew that the community could rely on, a small treasury produced by the preaching, the miracles, and faith.

Judas kept the money box into which offerings flowed, and these small amounts gave some hope, some public ambitions to certain members of the community. They spoke of Jesus as the king of Israel and became preoccupied with status, pre-eminence, favoritism, and all the ambitions and vanities of a takeover plot. In other words, everyone yearned for a position of importance over the kingdom that was to be theirs.

It's curious that Jesus chose Thomas, a nonbeliever, a man of everlasting doubts. But Jesus wanted him along, perhaps to show that he was not a despotic leader, intolerant of opposition. It almost seems that he was happy to have with him among his closest followers one who always regarded him with some suspicion, a skeptic, a nonbeliever, who, in following him, was forever oscillating between belief and unbelief—which probably makes the most accurate portrait of people of all times. We make choices that appear definitive, but they are arrived at along with the benefit and pain of doubt. Jesus' concern for doubt seems to me highly significant.

But, for my film—how was the difficult selection of these extraordinarily symbolic figures made?

We directors are not painters who need only a clean canvas to sketch an imaginary portrait of Peter, of Jesus, of Thomas. We have many actors to select from, but our choices are necessarily limited, we have to see who the current familiar faces are—the ones on the market, so to speak. You aren't dealing with an absolute choice but a relative one, which has to yield to a certain type of character, to the photography, to the reading of lines. In extreme cases you might be satisfied with the physical appearance and the eyes, but not the voice. Then you have to resort to another voice; you have to dub.

The typology of the groups that I assembled seemed to me quite satisfactory. They were all real, and even though they are actors of diverse origins and background—English, Italian, American, all professional actors—they worked together wonderfully. The casting of Judas was particularly difficult, almost agonizing, because everybody has his own image of this character.

It is for this reason—the image we all sketch in our fantasy—that you rarely succeed in satisfying everybody when you select a face to play a famous character. The actor I had in mind for many years was an Englishman, Ian McShane, who had a limited but interesting career. He is a man of charming personality and no complexes, quite a ladies' man, capable of practical jokes and truly traitorous deeds, all with a spirit, an elegance, and a vivacity that captivated all, even when he was completely in the wrong.

I studied the character thoroughly and made him a kind of radical with a very precise political vision—a man who knows everything, absolutely everything, except for the one thing that really mattered. For that reason, despite his careful calculating, despite his dream castle, the essential thing escaped him, namely, the flame, the flame of Jesus' love, the consuming flame of his mission, more important than all else, above petty scheming and earthly human logic. In fact, then, he understood nothing.

When finally everything collapses, a single phrase from Jesus suffices to repudiate him: "Not the mind, Judas, not the mind. Open your heart, open your eyes." Judas is prostrated by it. He knows he has missed it all.

Jesus wanted this type of man by his side, knowing well that they can betray. The intelligentsia who think they know all the answers, relying on reason alone, are the real traitors because they end up by betraying the very values that matter. Judas is not sinister, not a cutthroat, a killer for hire. He is a disciple, an enthusiast, a zealot even, but lacks the ardor to serve in that which is essential. In a word, he could wish you well but is not capable of loving you. At the end, faced with the burning flame of Jesus' total love, what is left for him but the noose? He has no alternative; his entire life, his way of existing, has been discredited. I see Judas very clearly in some current journalism. I find him in so many revolutions, the intransigent type, a pedant, so sure of himself, adept at scheming to advance error. I see him always there where the intellectual has manipulated or is again manipulating politics, ideologies, or the media. And it delights me that, with regard to Judas, Jesus pointed out that subtle and grave error of the human spirit, that unique *condemnation of the intelligence.* We are surrounded by Judases, and they are condemned to hang themselves, sooner or later, from the tree of their own pride.

John the Evangelist lived for seventy-four years. He belonged to that special species, the venerables, the patriarchs—those who had succeeded in going beyond the critical phase of youthful years. I didn't want him too young, so as not to magnify the sweetness that is intrinsic to his story; John, the beloved disciple, who Jesus looked upon almost as a son. There have even been scandalous accusations over the tenderness that Jesus showed toward this disciple. To avoid complications of this kind, I selected a very clean-cut young man with nothing of the adolescent about him. He is not Achilles' Patroclus, nor the ambivalent John of Leonardo.

For Peter, I chose the American James Farentino, well known on Television in America and frequently cast as a policeman. This good-natured man was perfect in the role of Peter, the angry disciple, quick to protest, displaying certain childish reactions, always upset and troubled, telling his companions: "Let me be, this man is too complicated for me. Why did you bring me to him?" And he has a row with his brother: "Don't put him in my way! You are used to John the Baptist, you are one who believes in these things. I am a fisherman, I believe in the nets, in my boats. Let me alone, leave me in peace. This man is upsetting our life."

But I portray him as a faithful dog that won't back away from danger. It growls but wags its tail, and finally runs after the danger like a summons it doesn't know how to resist.

There's a very beautiful moment in the film when Peter, out on the lake, sends his boats away. They are his whole life. To justify himself, he makes the excuse, "There are no fish this time of the year." Matthew, the more intelligent one, replies, "Why do you want to lie to yourself? You know better than I that you are lying, you know you will never return to Capernaum, you know very well you will never go back to drinking, to fishing . . . We will never be the same. The world will never be the same again. We know it . . . We are the first to know it."

Peter, as always, replies hesitantly, as though he doesn't understand, but he is already trembling because he senses within himself this budding desire to be on his way, this growing belief in Christ. I think that he might have been involved in frequent escapades, which Jesus tolerated. But Peter always came back. He was also quick to defend the Master, as when he cut off the ear of Malchus, a very revealing act, though it may be only legend.

Peter is a strong character, a pillar of strength. That is why, when Jesus asks all the disciples, "But who do you believe that I am?" and no one at that supreme moment had the courage to manifest his own thought, it is Peter alone who dared speak.

"You are the Messiah," he proclaims in a loud voice, uttering what a Hebrew would consider a blasphemy. It is the first time Jesus is proclaimed the Messiah. Profoundly moved, Jesus replies:

"Peter, you are blessed by God. Because flesh and blood have not revealed this to you, but the Spirit of my Father within you.

From here on I will call you Peter [Rock] and on this rock I will build what will become my church."

Thus Jesus hails him, the first man to have had the courage to proclaim him the Messiah. From that moment Jesus becomes for all of them the Messiah. It was Peter, the unruly one, the intemperate one, who roused them all, and who stamped that sublime story with the seal of recognition. And it will be Peter, the hapless one, who will deny him three times, deny his Messiah through fear, through cowardice, until he hears the cock crow.

Notes from a Journey in Tunisia:

The quality that most impresses me about this people, besides the kindness shown in their ready and genial hospitality, is their intelligence, their ability to size up a situation.

Respect for intelligence, above all other gifts, is typical of Mediterranean peoples. With good reason: the Gospel condemns anyone who calls his brother stupid.

Tunisia. We have decided to make Sousse and Monastir the two centers of our operation because this way we can count on the enclosed areas of the Temple and adjacent buildings in case of bad weather.

We will have to go through winter to the middle of April, or the last days of May 1976, to finish the filming.

It will be a long road; the local folk will be our companions, these desert nomads who crowd around our sets. We will have some difficulties with the women—the jealous attitude of their husbands for one, and (no small problem) their tattoos. Almost all Berber women have face, arms, and hands tattooed. There's no way of covering them with makeup, as it is a matter of magical symbols to protect against the Devil and forces of evil.

The old men will be another problem. Sixty percent of the population of Tunisia is under thirty years of age. Our assistants will have quite a task, looking for them from village to village and house to house.

Everything is looking good. Every scene has been settled. When we come back here, the characters who now live only on the pages of the script and in our fantasy will begin to stir and to live out the most beautiful and mysterious event mankind has ever known: the story of him who, as Alcuin says, in dying has shut off the road to death.

From a Notebook:

Bizerte, July 14, 1975

Lake Ishkeul, shallow but teeming with fish, is the nearest thing to the Gospel's Sea of Galilee. Surrounded by mountains and a very white countryside on the western border, it will recreate Capernaum beautifully, the fisherman's village, the birthplace of Peter and the other first disciples. For the village of Capernaum itself, I preferred Lamta, on the coast, not far from Monastir, a grouping of ancient stone houses on the bank of a lagoon exactly like a lake. The only serious problem will be that of transporting from north to south the boats that I had built at a shipyard in Tunisia, modeled after an ancient boat I had seen on the Nile.

At Monastir, near the celebrated *rabat,* we will construct our colossal Temple. Nearby, a veritable factory will arise, where our artisans, plasterers, sculptors, painters, carpenters, and masons will be working, alongside Tunisian craftsmen. The columns of the Temple will be made in Italy and shipped here. We have found that in Tunisia, where hotels and homes are being built at a frenetic pace, there is no tubular scaffolding, and plaster is scarce. For the first we will bring in a cargo ship from Genoa; for the second, a Tunisian factory has agreed to place its entire output at the exclusive disposition of our company.

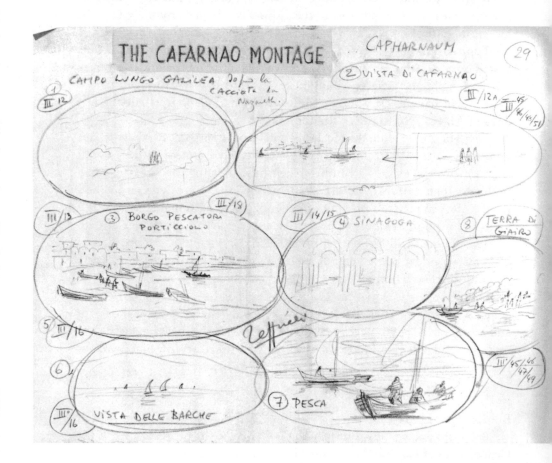

And so this monument, unequaled in the ancient world, and impossible to recapture today, or even suggest scenically in any existing architecture, will cast its great shadow upon the soft green grass of the meadow that surrounds the *rabat*. Another dream becomes a reality, if only in the fiction of a film.

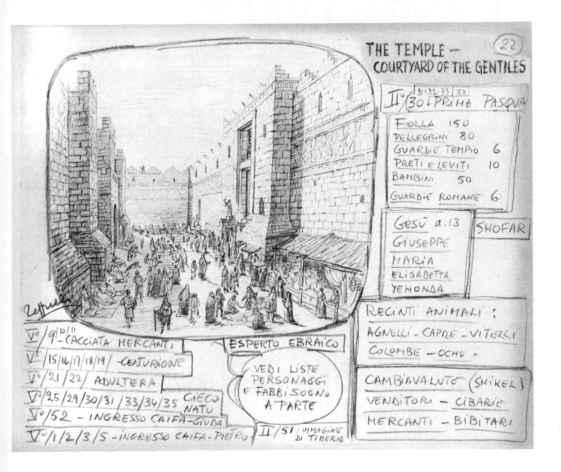

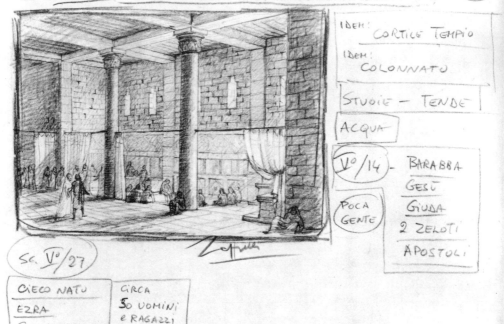

IDEM: CORTILE TEMPIO

IDEM: COLONNATO

STUOIE — TENDE

ACQUA

V°/14 - BARABBA

GESÙ

POCA GENTE — GIUDA

2 ZELOTI

APOSTOLI

SC. V°/27

CIECO NATO

EZRA

SAMUEL

1° UOMO

2° UOMO

CIRCA 50 UOMINI e RAGAZZI

CHAPTER 15

The Resurrection

Following the Gospel narrative, I shot a scene that, in cinematic terms, worked better than I had hoped. It was the one of the apostles right after Jesus' death. It shows their sorrow at the loss of a friend, of the Master, and their alarm at finding themselves in the eyes of a cyclone, as all of them could be suspected of complicity with Jesus and all might suffer the same fate.

Fearful, dismayed, hunted, and upset, they hide out.

While they are in hiding, unaware of what's going on, a scene like something out of a detective story takes place. The Sanhedrin fears Jesus even now in his death, and they have a huge stone placed in front of his tomb to thwart the disciples' expectation, learned from the Master, that, though he would die, after three days he would arise in glory.

A suspicion grips the Sanhedrin. Someone could run off with the body of the condemned and proclaim his resurrection. So, they take greater precautions, they wall up everything and seal it.

Even so, the corpse disappears.

The Sanhedrin knows that neither the apostles nor the Romans could have carried it away. Who, then? A rumor spreads in Jerusalem of the irrefutable fact of Jesus' Resurrection.

At this point in the film the public sees and hears accusations flying about from one to the others. By this time they know all the persons involved in the story of Christ and they ask, Who could have taken away the body? How was the stone removed despite the presence not only of the soldiers but also of the priests? But it happened. And the mystery of the victory of Jesus over death involves every viewer. If you do not accept the mystery of the Resurrection, neither can you accept Christianity.

The whole mission of Jesus was to overcome death in every meaning of the word, to overcome this world with its most inflexible rules, in order to bring us to our second birth.

While the disciples were in hiding, frightened and unable to find the courage to come out in the open and fulfill the command of Jesus, Mary Magdalene, with some other women, went to the tomb and found it empty. The body of the Master was not there. A gardener asks her, "Why are you crying?" Upset, her eyes filled with tears, she can't reply. She doesn't want to talk with anyone, but finally, touched by the man's kindness, she frantically begs him to tell her something about the disappearance of the Master's body.

Then she hears a voice: "Mary! Mary!" She recognizes the Master's voice. It is he, the gardener!

"Don't cling to me," Jesus enjoins. "I have not yet returned to my Father. But go, tell my disciples I have risen."

Magdalene then runs to look for the apostles. She finds them and enters their hideout, shouting: "He is risen, I saw him, I saw him with my own eyes."

As the Gospel records it, they simply do not believe her. They think she is a woman obsessed. Calm down, relax, they tell her. But she insists, it's true, it's true, I saw him, he is risen—a scene that Anne Bancroft played so marvelously.

Women's fantasies, says the disdainful Thomas, asking the others to confirm his disbelief. "James, do you believe it? And you, Matthew? And you, John, do you believe it?"

There's a silence, an awkward, thoughtful silence. Then Peter, coming to his feet, shouts, "I believe, because all that Jesus promised us has come about."

"What's this? You! You who denied him three times?" Thomas laughs in his face.

"Yes, I am a coward, a traitor. But we have all betrayed him, not only Judas. The Romans didn't know him, even our own Sanhedrin didn't know him, those who condemned him. But we, yes, we who lived with him and ate with him, we knew him. We knew he was the Son of God, yet we have betrayed him, all of us, all of us together!"

And then Peter, the apostle most prone to discouragement, but whose faith was most vibrant, professes his conviction that Jesus is risen.

"I know in my heart that the Master has forgiven me, that he has forgiven us, all of us."

After this confession of Peter's, I was to shoot the scene of the return of the risen Jesus to the apostles. In fact, in Morocco, I had already set up the entire scene.

The first indications that we were not on the right path came from the makeup and wardrobe department. Otello Fawa, our makeup man, who had wholeheartedly contributed so much to the outer realization of the characters, came to me a bit upset and asked for some definite suggestions about Powell's makeup, because, for the first time, he found himself utterly baffled. At the same time, Escoffier and Sabbatini expressed their perplexity about the costume Jesus should wear: torn and tattered? the red cape of the Passion? the shroud? a new tunic?

Immediately Nannuzzi, infinitely resourceful even in the most impossible situations, confided sad-eyed that he could find no way to solve the lighting problem in this scene. And finally Powell himself seemed absolutely devoid of the inner strength and store of ideas that had enabled him to surmount so many other difficulties.

Since the time at our disposal was so limited, I mustered up my courage and decided on a solution. And we all got ready to shoot.

The scene had been set up in this way: After Peter's dramatic confession, which enlightened the apostles, overcoming the doubts still in their hearts, a moment of mystical tension would have to be created and Jesus would appear at the door left open by Magdalene. A nail-pierced hand would be the first shot.

At this point a wave of fear, of incredulity and discomfort comes over the apostles and they draw back like frightened animals. But Jesus approaches them and one by one reassures them, calling them by name and overcoming Thomas's resistance by urging him to put his hand on his wounds.

He directs harsh words to Thomas, according to the Gospel: "You believe because you have touched me and seen me," and turning to Peter, he says, "Blessed are they who believe without having seen."

To write this scene, or to recount it, is undeniably effective. But on film it lacked all credibility and veered our project toward the perilous shores of a Hollywood epic. This was precisely what we had been trying to avoid. And so, taking upon myself the discouragement and dejection of everybody involved, I decided to suspend filming and take some time for reflection.

Meanwhile our calendar indicated implacably that our final days of filming in Morocco were fast approaching. So I decided that we would reshoot the scene during the last two days before our departure for Tunisia.

They were anxious days for me. I was cruelly aware of my powerlessness in the face of problems so much greater than I might be capable of solving. And I was aware of the tenuousness of my faith.

Labella was in Tunisia. I phoned him in desperation and asked him to come and share the problem as he had done so often in critical moments of the film. He arrived on the first flight available, and we spent hours and hours of a sleepless night trying to find a solution. Finally, we decided on another approach.

Jesus returns as a friend, a friend distressed because he needs the love of his disciples. He is not immediately recognizable, like the traveler who appears to the two disciples on the road to Emmaus.

The idea appealed to us and excited us. It appealed to Powell, too, and Nannuzzi, the makeup department—everybody.

On the next to last day at Meknes we were on the set, lights were positioned, cameras readied, the scene with the apostles rehearsed. We were only waiting for Powell to arrive.

In the normally bright and limpid skies of Meknes that morning, a yellow streak slashed across the horizon. The local people gazed at it apprehensively. We couldn't understand what they were saying, but some of the older people were shaking their heads. At eleven o'clock, when we were ready to film the scene, the sky suddenly darkened and all of Meknes seemed immersed in a dense yellow mist. A hot, violent wind swept through the whole countryside, uprooting thousands of olive trees, ripping roofs off thatched huts and houses.

Our set had been built in the open, and all the Moroccan and Italian workmen were hurriedly beginning to secure the structures, and the electricians to anchor the outdoor lights with steel cables. Powell, who had taken refuge in a doorway, was blasted by wind and sand, and most of the large windows of the hotel were shattered.

We were all holding our breath, frozen by an almost infantile terror. That was when I said, "That's it. Enough of this scene! Evidently it is not right that we shoot it this way." From that moment on, the Resurrection scene remained an unkept appointment.

For me it was an admission of defeat, or a secret lesson, a reminder of the limits of my profession and powers of inspiration. It was a surrender, the only one that scathed me in an enterprise otherwise so totally rewarding.

CHAPTER 16

The Pietà

Poor Olivia! The most anguishing scene of them all was that of the "Pietà," the great scene of the Descent from the Cross. I had a clear picture in mind, but no one could imagine what would actually happen. Behind the little hill of my Golgotha I had placed powerful water pumps by a murky, muddy pool. We actually showered the poor actors with a dirty, dark, reddish rain that nevertheless had a chromatic and dramatic effect.

I had set up all the effects, including the powerful smoke machines to produce the heavy clouds that had to darken the sky. Of course, the four cameras were positioned, the dollies, too, and the crane. For an entire day a long and difficult series of the scene's sequences had been rehearsed for filming at the very moment of sunset—the sequence of the Descent with the executioners routinely removing the nails, releasing the body, and throwing it to the ground; the Roman officer who has to make sure that Jesus is dead, ready to dispatch him were he still alive.

Then, waiting for the sunset, we took a brief break.

At last the light was just right, everybody ready, Olivia in a total trance, the weeping Tunisian women around her, and Powell, poor fellow, up there on the cross. The arc lamps are lighted, the hoses are opened, and we begin to film the grand scene. And action begins.

The executioners remove one of the thieves and give him to his aged mother. The other they just cast aside.

Something extraordinary, almost apocalyptic, happens with Powell up there on the cross, heroic under that icy, dirty water in the middle of February. They take down his body and lay it out on the ground like a rag. The Roman officer kicks him to be sure he is dead and calls the women to hurry it up. The Romans have had enough of all this and want to return to their barracks as soon as possible to dry off after that torrential rain. Moreover it is still dusk, the sunset before the vigil of Passover, and the Jews, too, would want the punishment over and done with as soon as possible so the Passover Sabbath could begin.

Then Olivia, supported by two women, comes into the scene and throws herself on the body of Jesus. At that instant, a Tunisian woman, taken by panic or emotion, stood right in front of one of the cameras. With a strong pull we succeeded in getting her out of the way while the cameras continued to film Olivia, who was performing prodigiously, in a state of superhuman desperation. In a few minutes the scene was over.

Stop. A short break.

We carried Olivia off in total shock. We remount everything, we change costumes, the makeup man restores all poor Powell's wounds, which had been washed away by the rain. The film's doctor gives him a camphor injection because he is no longer able to stand (he had to lie supine, rain battering his stomach, without breathing, the cameras over him on a closeup, and water running into his nose to the point of suffocation). We had to do it all over again because of the Tunisian woman standing in front of the camera and because of a rain-drenched lens.

Everybody to his station! They go to call Olivia and find her in a pitiful condition, because, after that tremendous tension, someone had charitably given her a small glass of cognac. Her nerves were jumping, and she couldn't control herself. She threw herself on the ground, screamed, seemed possessed, insane, releasing all her tension. Finally, bewildered, she began to laugh, to laugh uncontrollably.

I tried to bring her to her senses, concerned about the spectacle she was making and about Powell and Miss Bancroft's state of nerves—in fact, everybody's at this point. But poor Olivia didn't hear me.

We decided, however, to carry her there, almost like a sack, and place her in front of the camera. Miss Bancroft, suddenly overcome seeing Olivia stumbling, laughing, shouting, falling to her knees, lost control and began to slap her, shouting: "That's enough. We can't go on like this. You are ruining everything, you are being irresponsible!"

The rain began again with Powell, up there on the cross, pelted with muddy, icy water. They take him down again and lay him on the ground. And finally, we were able to drag in Olivia and throw her on the body of Jesus. She lay there, trembling.

When it was all over, this desperate scene was so effective (the mother collapsed on the body of her son, clasping him as though they were sleeping together in the rain) that we decided to keep it in the film.

CHAPTER 17

Did Judas Betray?

The Last Supper sequence, originally to be filmed in the same place as the Resurrection scenes, was postponed to our Tunisian period.

Unfortunately, it seemed necessary to rebuild the set, but instead, when we arrived at Monastir, we discovered a perfect place for the Last Supper, a small courtyard, needing only roof beams and straw, like the humble rooms of houses in Jerusalem.

So, with no further complications or delays, we were ready to shoot this scene that I felt had to be one of the most compelling in the film. Actually, although we had set it up right down to the last detail according to the traditional Jewish ritual (it couldn't be otherwise, because, as I will never tire of saying, Jesus and the apostles were Jews from head to toe), it marked the moment when Jesus superseded the ancient rite and gave his disciples and all humanity the Eucharistic mystery.

We were finally ready to shoot. Within these humble walls, this simple room, the atmosphere was just right. I became aware that in the move from Morocco to Tunisia my concept of this and other scenes had matured. The sequence opened with festive singing. The Passover for the Jews was very much like the spirit of Christmas for us. It was a yearly feast for the people and for families reunited to celebrate the liberation of their ancestors from Egypt. There were the children; there was the vacant seat for Elijah, the awaited prophet, who could return at any moment. Everyone sang and danced in an atmosphere of joy.

And there are our friends, these "conspirators," outlawed by now, and at this moment in serious danger, coming together secretly to celebrate the Passover with Jesus.

The Sanhedrin knew perfectly well that the apostles had to get out of Jerusalem at night because it had become too dangerous for them and the Master, but they also knew that this night they would stay in the city. They were in touch with Judas, who had a very definite plan, namely, to bring Jesus before the Sanhedrin for a clarification that, to his thinking, would resolve everything.

And when, during the supper, Jesus turns to him and in a low voice says, "What you have to do, do quickly." Judas believes that with these words he has the Master's approval to go ahead with his plan, and he leaves the room, relieved of all doubts. "The Master knows and approves," he thinks to himself.

Of all the disciples, Judas is perhaps the one who most engaged my fancy and my curiosity as a film director.

Did Judas really betray? And if so, why? Was a betrayal necessary? Is there any logic to the Gospel account or is it simply a dramatic addition—a device to justify the arrest of Jesus?

A great Catholic theologian writes: "All textual difficulties and all the particularized problems of the Gospels appear insignificant before the great moral problem we face in Judas's fall and betrayal."

Mark doesn't even try to explain Judas's act, he merely suggests greed as a motive. Judas sells Christ for thirty pieces of silver. The other evangelists make no mention of the motive for such villainy. Luke's hypothesis and John's—that he was obsessed or possessed— leaves much unsolved. Was his motive ambition, or envy of Peter and John, who were the most beloved of the apostles? Or fear provoked by the collapse of Christ's plans and constantly increasing dangers?

But putting them all together—greed, ambition, jealousy, fear, distrust—and magnifying them in the tension of the moment, the betrayal does not appear sufficiently motivated. It seems pointless, to say the least.

Many have chosen to see in Judas the personification of an unbelieving, perfidious Judaism, Satan incarnate, who seemed at a certain moment to conquer Christ. He can also be perceived as the embodiment of an early tradition according to which Jesus' death was the work of the Jews who delivered him over to Pilate.

Judas never did anything haphazardly; he planned his action carefully. We tried to indicate this through Zerah, a scribe of the Sanhedrin, a key character in the development of the drama, played superbly by the Shakespearean actor Ian Holm. Zerah would be Stalin's Yagoda, Hitler's Himmler, Napoleon's Fouché.

In every power system there is always a Zerah, the secular arm, the executor. In my script I fancy that there was a Zerah to guide Judas, making him think that the destiny of Jesus was in his hands, hoping it would appeal to his political ambitions.

Judas went to Zerah to inform him of Jesus' arrival in Jerusalm. In his mind the moment had come to make the prophet known to the fathers of Israel, as a man on the verge of liberating the nation from slavery.

"He is without doubt an interesting man," the scribe tells him, "he has remarkable views. I have heard also that he raises the dead to life, that he performs miracles. Surely we in Israel have had many prophets, perhaps too many. It remains to be seen whether he is inspired by God or the Devil. We have to see, my friend, we have to follow him closely . . ."

Judas is delighted at having brought Jesus to the attention of this important pawn. But from that moment on, Jesus begins to dash Judas's hopes, to frustrate his ingenious plans. He arrives at the Temple and drives out the idlers, the merchants, the profiteers; he breaks up everything, he attacks the Pharisees. "What have you done to the house of the Lord?" he thunders. "Jerusalem was the queen of the world, now she is a whore." Then he frees the animals from their pens and yells to the priests to forget their vain, useless offerings. "God doesn't want sacrifices of bulls or goats, he wants purity of heart."

On Thursday of Passover week, a final spectacular gesture scandalized the Pharisees. Jesus healed the man blind from birth.

Among all the miraculous healings of the crippled, the sick, Christ chose for his last miracle the healing of the man born blind —to my mind a most symbolic act. Jesus cures the blind man for a very definite purpose, so that he may see the world, know it, judge it, and then make a choice. The blind man will receive his sight to decide whether he will be for God or for the Devil. One who doesn't see is not responsible either for his virtues or his sins.

Jesus frequently met this man begging at the Temple gate. I picture him seeing the man, studying him at times, and one day deciding to heal him. The poor fellow, long resigned to his pitiful condition, rebels. He doesn't want to be touched, he protests. But

Jesus, mixing dust and saliva, rubs his eyes and cures him. He asks the astonished man: "Now that you can see, tell me, do you believe in the Son of Man?"

"Tell me who he is," the bewildered man stammers, "so that I may believe."

"He who stands before you," Jesus says. And the man finally seems to understand that Jesus has opened his eyes in order to open his mind in a conscious act of faith. Falling to his knees, he murmurs: "It is you."

This scene, one of the most extraordinary in the Gospels, is recounted by John with the skill of a dramatist, and I am sorry—as with the episode of Lazarus so masterfully portrayed by John—that I wasn't able, for lack of space, to tell it in its entirety.

Some Pharisees standing nearby saw what happened, and heard those words, truly blasphemous in their ears. They decided to intervene. This man, they asserted, wasn't blind. He pretended blindness to appeal to the sympathy of the Temple faithful and earn himself a living. When he opened his eyes he simply collaborated with a hoaxer, the Nazarene.

At this point Jesus explodes in one of his rare but awesome invectives: "Woe to you, Scribes and Pharisees, hypocrites!"

Jesus' defiance climaxes with the proclamation of his identity with the Father and with the announcement that he will not return among them in the Temple until they have learned to greet him with the cry: "Blessed is he who comes in the name of the Lord. Because my Father and I are one."

This astonishing declaration unleashes a tumult in the Temple; tempers flash, consciences are offended. The situation becomes explosive, and the Romans, who were on the alert as always during the Passover, were ready to take advantage of any pretext to intervene.

Let's not forget that there were two hundred thousand or more pilgrims in the city, all charged with a mystic exaltation, accentuated by ther awareness of the force of their numbers and their faith.

After Jesus' attack on the Pharisees, tension reached the limits of the guards' tolerance, and the Sanhedrin found itself obliged to take measures to remove him from circulation, because he had now become exceedingly dangerous. And here Judas returns to the scene.

In my account, I repeat, Judas had devised an apparently flawless plan to save the Master: bring him to the Sanhedrin, persuade him to confront the doctors of the Law and the authority of the state. The confrontation would surely turn out to be a triumph for him. The Sanhedrin would understand Jesus and use him to reach an entente with the Romans.

The Gospel itself gives us the key to Judas's character, this disciple who relied more on reason than the heart to understand Jesus. The Gospel says: "When Judas learned that the Sanhedrin had condemned Jesus, he was filled with remorse and killed himself." He killed himself, therefore, because he didn't expect the Master to be condemned. He killed himself because he realized, only then, that he had betrayed him.

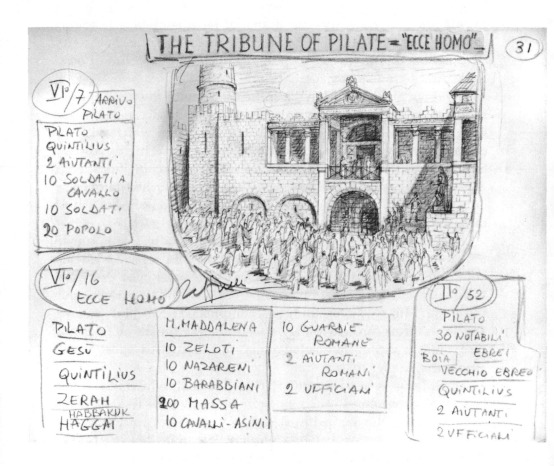

CHAPTER 18

The Final Sacrifice

Events now move swiftly—the drama of Jesus is rushing headlong toward human tragedy. The Master and the apostles leave the city that night and retire to a safe place by a well on the mount of olive trees. And here Christ's agony begins.

I was not able to develop the entire scene, with the three appeals to the apostles who, drowsy from food and wine, are sleeping like weary sheep. Jesus tries to wake them: "Can't you watch with me even for an hour?" And so, in the silence of the night, scarcely broken by the rustle of wind, we come to the kiss of Judas.

Why the baseness of a kiss? Why exactly must the traitor carry out his wicked deed at the very moment of the Son of Man's most intense consternation?

First of all, Judas brings the guards to a remote place, known only to him and his outlaw companions. If the soldiers had suddenly appeared with their torches, they would have awakened everyone, and the apostles and other followers of Jesus would have then given the alarm. This way everything is accomplished in absolute silence, and Jesus offers himself to his persecutors like the Lamb of Scripture. He is a victim immolated alone, forbidding his apostles any attempt whatever to save him.

With Jesus' arrest we come to Peter's denial, which in the film had to be compressed into a single incident. While Jesus is being condemned by the Sanhedrin at early dawn, the people, with that facility mobs have for changing allegiance in an instant at a turn of events, begin to alter their attitude toward Jesus.

This Master who had so agitated the country, who even at Passover time had turned Jerusalem upside down—stirring up ev-

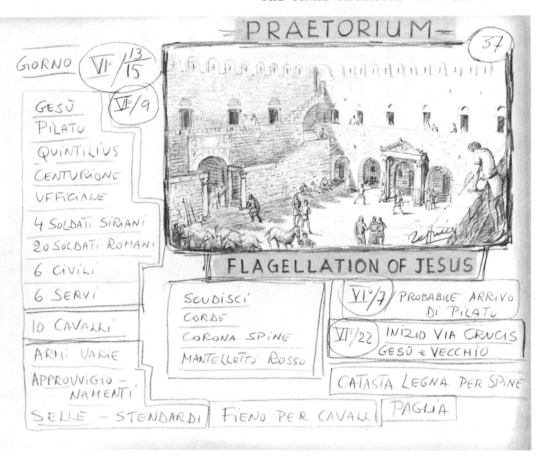

erybody's conscience—and who had promised the Kingdom, let himself be taken with no resistance, without a word, without a threat. In a word, Jesus betrayed everybody who had put their faith in him. This is how his followers began to think.

Peter himself, so aggressive, so pugnacious, so quarrelsome, being recognized by a young woman and caught in a group of fanatics who also recognize him, is cornered. Now, in a scene of great confusion, terrified of being arrested and condemned, he parries, raises his shoulders, shudders, and says, "But I . . . I have never known this Jesus you're talking about." At that very moment the cock crows. And at the same instant, outside the walls, alone with his desperate remorse, Judas hangs himself.

In arranging the succession of that night's events in Jerusalem and picturing to myself a dramatic sequence that could bring together all the characters involved in Jesus' downfall, I thought of establishing parallel destinies for the two apostles who represent opposite poles among Jesus' followers: Peter and Judas.

In terms of editing and defining the action for both of them at the same moment, as dawn breaks they are going away from us, from the camera, from the place where Jesus is a prisoner—each with his own despair. Peter wants to find pardon, and Judas, a tree.

CHAPTER 19

The Music

As soon as I finished shooting the film, in the middle of June, I did a provisional edit. Then our work began: The final touches, the selections, the decisions, the cuts. Some episodes were weak, some just right; some needed more space, some less.

The last phase has to do with the music. Music can be determined only after the playing time of the film has been decided. And when it has been fused with the film, as supporting sound, you cannot change a thing, because the music establishes the tempo, the rhythm, the pace. The music is the final seal that separates the director from his creation.

When the editing has been completed, you turn your scenes over to a composer who begins to work on it. Then he conducts it and records it. The total result is probably tried again. Where necessary it is polished up. It is tried once more, until finally the music takes definitive shape. From that moment on, as I have said, the film crystallizes; it has its own autonomous life.

Your own creation, totally emancipated from you, now, starts to face its destiny. And so also a part of our life comes to an end, the fatigues of filming, the concern in keeping every scene firmly in hand, every part, every face, every word—it is all over. The storms and tensions of creation subside, and music carries it off, sweeps it all away.

It is a serious moment, a painful moment. When I heard the music of the Crucifixion and we had put it onto the film, I went back months, years, plunged into an abyss of memories.

I returned cleansed of all those experiences, beautiful and fearful at the same time, and I looked at the film as though I were seeing it for the first time.

Because it is a definitive seal, the music is a delicate element. It can jeopardize the work (as often happens) if it does not complement the spirit of the film.

Many of my colleagues are content to take musical passages from records, using quartets, sonatas, or symphonies, putting together a collection of cultural excerpts but forgetting that, in a film, the music is a parallel discourse, a conversation, not a passive discourse. It is a living force that collaborates, that penetrates to the very heart of the film.

I could choose from among many great musicians. Among them was the name of Maurice Jarre, a composer I had been following for many years.

Jarre, a young man, had written for the Theatre National Populaire with Vilar. While hardly more than a boy he composed the scores for *The Cid* and Gérard Philipe's *Lorenzaccio.* He began as a percussionist and from the very first showed extraordinary talent. Swept along on a wave of success, he composed such highly popular scores as those that accompanied *The Bridge on the River Kwai* and *Doctor Zhivago,* commercial films to which, nevertheless, Jarre's music made an unmistakable contribution.

In his career he has ranged from great commercial successes to others less publicized but artistically masterful.

My secret hope was that, if the mysterious force that bewitched so many who took part in the film could be aroused in him, too, Jarre would be just the artist to furnish me with a splendid score. The result is melodic music, despite the emotional violence of a huge percussion section, and very skillful music that obeys all the laws of the game, marked by technically valuable insights.

Jarre went to work on the film in June 1976. He spent his vacation at home, after having seen some phases of the editing with me and having discussed every aspect of the film. For example, for the scene of the miraculous multiplication of the fish, which I had filmed with extreme care because the idea of showing a mass of agonized fish was repugnant to me. I relied on the music to suggest the image of the fish, caught in the nets, collected in baskets, and offered to the people. In this case the music performed a veritable miracle with flowing, liquid, transparent sonorities. On the other hand, the Way of the Cross is commented upon, animated, and embellished by a heavy, provocative passage full of surprising blendings of sound, supported by a wealth of rhythm and a fury of the percussion—harsh and disturbing sonorities over which, from time to time, an exalted but mournful theme emerges—a funereal but at the same time triumphant march.

With the patience of a monk, Jarre researched the documents and musical texts of the ancient Jewish tradition. He studied the poetic structure of the psalms for hints of possible musical cadences. He uncovered archaic instruments; others, he recreated, such as the *aulos,* a flute that the apostle Thaddeus plays.

From a Note on the Plans for the Crucifixion Sequence:

> On Golgotha, in view of the walls of Jerusalem, a menacing scaffold stood as a constant warning to anyone daring to defy Rome's law. . . . Jesus will carry on his shoulders only the transverse bar of the Cross, what the Romans called the *patibulum* and which was set into the *stipes,* or vertical beam, which was already implanted at the place of execution.

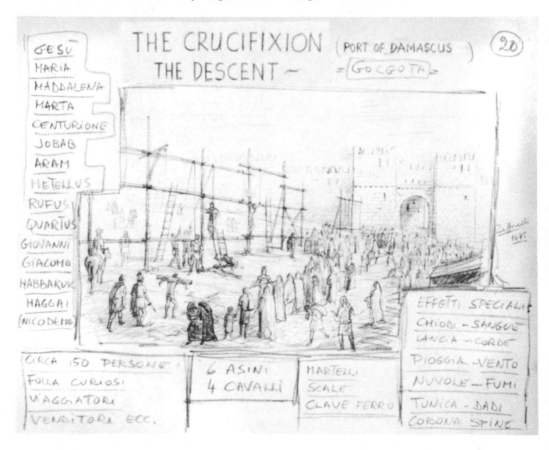

It was necessary to prepare the *titulus*—the shingle to be affixed to the top of the cross with the words "Jesus of Nazareth, King of the Jews," written in Aramaic, Latin, and Greek. For this and for the other two condemned men, we must rely on the knowledge of Monsignor Rossano.

I remember seeing in a base-relief at Santa Sabina an unusual representation of the Crucifixion that appears to me to correspond to the probable historical reality. I must discuss it with Labella.

CHAPTER 20

Now It All Begins

And so my film went away. I watched it depart.

It left like a son who has married. He leaves and you can't hold him back. Now this film that has so deeply absorbed me, and perhaps still more profoundly marked me, begins to make its own way.

Discussion of the film still goes on, about its significance, its true intentions, which were to offer a little faith to today's troubled world.

It can only give so much, as you can't expect a film to brush aside —despite all our sincere best efforts—the uncertainties and doubts that textual criticism continues to raise about the figure of Jesus and about the Gospels and that laxity, hedonism, and the easy cynicism of this distressed epoch never cease to nurture.

Reading such texts—and there are thousands of them—and hearing the most corrosive comments, the suspicion can arise that the vast structure of Christianity was born of nothing, of a misunderstanding, of a basic moral and spiritual need of the period, of the convictions of a community, which were reflected in the unique figure of the Master, Christ.

An invention, then? What a marvelous invention, that has so often succeeded in enlightening humanity, that has an ability to convert barbarians, turn people of every race to love and purity, convince the worst of us to repent, and sow in the human heart the seed of goodness.

Still there are those who continue to dedicate themselves to shattering the Gospel by declaring it "editorialized"—in their kindest comments. They more often accuse many superb passages in the New Testament of being apocryphal, to the point of suggesting that they are badly contrived. Jesus himself was only a name, a fantasy —just a myth!

Is it possible that this sublime story, which they claim was put together by a group of Jews, could have lasted for centuries and conquered the entire world by the message it conveys? a message adapting itself, without betraying its basic rigor, to every civilization, every age, to every race, so rich is it in secret powers? And when it seems on the verge of being toppled and perishing, see how it arises stronger than ever, with a brilliance never before appreciated. See it dispense new hope, fresh consolation, new love.

It has been a burning mystery locked in the depths of Jesus' mission on earth that hovers over us, calls and accompanies us—the mystery, perhaps, of his own boundless grandeur. If we take up the Gospel and read it in trusting humility and open sincerity, we find the shattered and scattered pieces of the mosaic, so violated and ruined by criticism, bringing themselves together miraculously in a marvelous picture, recovering the dimensions of a pure, necessary truth.

The film is on its way, and I don't know, even now that all the tension has relaxed and weariness set in, whether I have created a distinguished film or not. But if a single showing of my film succeeds in stimulating one person, awakening in him or her an echo of that divine message that each of us carries within, not only will I have justified all the sacrifices made, but I will have given an enlarged meaning and scope to my entire life.

Postscript

The book is almost entirely printed when an excited phone call comes in from Zeffirelli asking if there is still time to change a chapter—the one in which he speaks of his bitterness over the forced abandonment of the script's Resurrection scene. I reply that the book has been printed, that we are in the process of binding it, that it is impossible to change it. Zeffirelli insists, he protests, he implores.

Let us acknowledge how important it is that the book should conclude with a solution to the problem that was the most agonizing in all the months of filming, a conscientious scruple, one that he called his shame, his surrender, that he was unequal to the task of representing the Resurrection.

A few days before delivering the finished print of the film, right there on the deadline, Zeffirelli started to rummage through the hundred and thirty hours of footage in a desperate search for a solution. He told me that, having spent the night on the moviola with his cutter, Reginald Mills, at exactly 5:00 A.M. he found a photographic test of Jesus' leave taking of the disciples after the Resurrection, a test shot a Meknes in the apostles' hideaway, forgotten in that enormous heap of material. Suddenly, everything turned around: those few feet of film offered the simplest solution, honest and clear. It is the consoling farewell of Jesus to his disciples and to us all, and his exhortation not to fear, since he is with us for all days until the end of time.

The joy of recovery was soon followed by a worry that the test might exist only in a positive print and that the negative, along with those of so many other tests, had been sent to the shredder. After waking up at that hour the foreman of the processing and printing establishment, and after a frantic search, the existence of the negative, in perfect condition, was confirmed.

The scene is now in the film, and among its other merits, it contains a phrase that has always been dear to Zeffirelli's heart, spoken by the disciple at Emmaus: "Stay with us, Lord, it is evening and the day is already over."

TIZIANO BARBIERI
Editor, the Italian edition